A Cup of Sin

Middle East Literature in Translation
Michael Beard, Series Editor

A Cup of Sin

Selected Poems

Simin Behbahani

Edited and Translated from the Persian
by Farzaneh Milani and Kaveh Safa

With Introductory Essays by the Poet and
an Afterword by Kaveh Safa

Syracuse University Press

Library of Congress Cataloging-in-Publication Data

Bihbihānī, Sīmīn.
[Poems. English. Selections]
A cup of sin : selected poems/Simin Behbahani; edited and translated
from the Persian by Farzaneh Milani and Kaveh Safa; with introductory
essays by the poet and an afterword by Kaveh Safa.
p. cm.—(Middle East literature in translation)
ISBN 0-8156-0554-4 (cloth : alk. paper)
1. Bihbihānī, Sīmīn—Translations into English.
I. Milani, Farzaneh. II. Safa, Kaveh. III. Title. IV. Series.
PK6561.B5A24 1999
891'.5513—dc21 98-53791

Manufactured in the United States of America

Contents

The Poems

Contents

⑥

Contents

Contents

❧

Contents
❧

Farzaneh Milani teaches Persian language and literature and women's studies at the University of Virginia in Charlottesville. She is the author of *Veils and Words: The Emerging Voices of Iranian Women Writers* (Syracuse University Press and I. B. Taurus) and has also served as guest editor for two special issues of *Nimeye Digar* on Simin Daneshvar and Simin Behbahani.

Kaveh Safa has taught courses in anthropology at City Colleges in New York and Los Angeles and at the University of Memphis, and in Persian language and literature at the universities of Virginia and Chicago. His current teaching and research interests are in poetics and sexuality and gender. He is completing a dissertation on concepts of masculinity in Iranian culture for the Department of Anthropology at the University of Chicago.

Preface

I t is in the endings of these poems where you really start to hear her voice. Sometimes the concluding lines add an extra element, like the bump at the end of a long descent that throws your sled momentarily into the air. The exit lines may look back at what she has said and recapitulate. Sometimes they sound like a retraction:

> My tongue has strayed like a broken pen.
> My trace dissolves like ink in water.
>> ("Mind: Smoke Rings")

[Pareh pareh shod zaban-am, hamchu khameh-ye shekasteh
Pas bar ab shod neshanam, chun morakkab-e zodudeh.]

The ending may repeat word for word the opening phrases of the poem in the manner of a motif in music:

> I mean, to pay homage to being, you must sing.
>> ("Gypsiesque [13]")

[Yaʾni be hormat-e budan bayad tarneh bekhani.]

Sometimes the concluding lines seem mysteriously suspended, detached from the rest of the poem, a statement which doesn't exactly sum things up but takes a step back, sketching a space and forcing the reader to look back across the gap to remind ourselves where we have been. In one poem we start at the scene of a flogging and end up at the scene of writing, watching now from the poet's writing desk:

> From deep oblivion, an agitation, a gaze . . .
> Myself. My desk. My office.
> Myself. Ceiling. Wall.
>> ("Flog!")

[Ze zharfa-ye nesyan, talashi, negahi . . .
man-o miz-o daftar, man-o saqf-o divar.]

Again and again you hear a conscious gesture of variation, a continued
expenditure of energy to the very last word. Her poems never coast to a
stop, nor do they strain for a loud climactic reprise. There isn't anything
much like it in western poetry, though Shakespeare's sonnets sometimes
end with a couplet that breaks free and floats off at a comparable slight dis-
tance from the rest of the poem. The Iranian reader, however, will see
exactly where it comes from. Every poet worth reading has a particular
weight and texture that recurs like a signature, recognizable diction or a pri-
vate language, a characteristic sequence of ideas which distributes images
or information through the poem, favored sounds or allusions. What marks
the weave of Simin Behbahani's poetry is a familiar traditional pattern,
unspoken, which the Iranian reader observes tacitly behind the poem. It
may be so familiar that there is no need to be particularly aware of it. This
is the pattern of the ghazal, a form so widespread that it is virtually syn-
onymous in Persian with lyric poetry. American and European readers need
to look for it in literary encyclopedias, where they find a list of specifications
that may seem arbitrary: a single rhyme throughout, a tendency to keep
each rhymed component syntactically separate, so that a little space sur-
rounds each pair of lines, and a conclusion in which the poem's voice turns
back to address the writing self by pen-name ("Hafez, you have written a
ghazal as difficult as piercing a hole through a pearl"; "O Saʾdi don't com-
plain if they call you crazy"). It is this last moment, where the poem curls
up out of its own discursive universe and looks back, which imparts its dis-
tinctive feeling of closure. It is perhaps the most readily translated of all the
ghazal's effects. And sometimes Behbahani's closing lines are very much in
the classical form:

> You're the hope in the heart of Simin-the-broken-hearted,
> put an end to my misery, come.
> ("Wine of Light")

[Omid-e khater-e Simin-e del shekasteh toʾi;
mara nakhah az in bish na-omid. Biya.]

The traditional elements are the ones American readers are least equipped
to appreciate. Our eyes are trained to see the break with the past, and this
applies to institutions other than poetry. To outside observers, twentieth-
century political Iran has been unlucky altogether. One shift of power after
another has disappointed its own supporters—the Constitutional Revolu-
tion, the coup of Reza Shah, the movement around Mosaddeq and the rev-
olution of 1979. We forget that there is a resilient civilization which persists

through all these changes. A country remains, and its citizens fashion networks of daily life that are independent of what we see in the newspaper, poetry being one of the institutions that survives. We may think of Simin Behbahani as one of the poets of daily life who has found her way to negotiate the public space whatever its restrictions, to wear that veil out into the street, to claim her own distinctive voice without being drowned out. Often (as in "Flog!" or "You Said, It's Only Grapes") she is an outspoken observer of the social scene. And she is regularly an ingenious reworker of an ongoing dialogue of modern poets.

Something American readers might not suspect is that women poets have been dominant figures in modern Iran. Parvin E³tesami (1907–1941), whose homiletic poetry explored new possibilities in traditional forms, is one of the major voices in the anthologies. Foruq Farrokhzad (1934–1967), whose independent and sometimes flamboyant life, as recorded in an elegant confessional poetry, followed something we may think of as a western model. E³tesami's poetry is a great challenge to the English translator; Farrokhzad's translates so readily into English that there has been one readable edition after another. Simin Behbahani occupies a space between. Her commitment and passion come across directly, but her relation to the past of Persian poetry requires an unusual sensitivity to catch, even to hint at in English. And she has been very fortunate indeed in her translators, who have managed again and again to identify the current that flows through the poem where another translator might have been trapped in its word-to-word information. When you compare texts, you feel that their attention never lags; you feel rather than see them reassembling and rethinking. Even when the text flirts with the inarticulate, the English recreates the feeling and rhythm with uncanny precision:

> Must write something, must, but where?
> To find a notebook or tablet, where?
> ("Must Write Something")

> [Bayad chizi nevesht. — Bayad, amma koja
> Luhi ya daftari digar ba ma koja?]

Behbahani is a poet whose honesty goes right down to the details of her search for the right word, the pen in hand and the thought spiraling inward to express itself, a close observer, a poet with technical precision and a heart. And the heart beats in English as well.

Michael Beard

Grand Forks, North Dakota

November 11, 1998

Acknowledgments

❦

Most of all, the translators owe thanks to Simin Behbahani not only for writing poems well worth the translators' six-year labor of love but for her help and encouragement in translating them. By patiently responding to the translators' queries, she has in effect held their hands as they braved (otherwise too timidly or blindly) many a chasm, mountain pass, and bridge that separates and connects persons and poems, languages, literary traditions, cultures, and histories. Of course, this is not to make her responsible for their slips and falls but to acknowledge her help in the distance traveled. What a privilege, this hand-holding with a living poet, especially on occasions when translating feels less like walking a bridge than walking a tightrope through patches of fog and darkness. How deprived are translators for whom the author is dead—physically, psychologically, intellectually, or aesthetically. How depraved, when they kill her off intentionally. How pitiful, when they celebrate this death or murder.

Let us clarify what we as translators mean by this privilege with a few examples. Consider the propensity in modern Persian poetry (whether by necessity, force of habit, or choice) for oblique figurative expression—for example, "skewered nightingales" standing for silenced or censored poets, or dogs giving up their freedom standing for political and moral compromise, or "dark and stormy nights" serving as barometers for political, moral, and cultural oppression. It made all the difference for the poet to encourage her translators sometimes to interpret her poems against the grain, stressing the concrete over the abstract, the particular over the general, the historical over the timeless, the literal over the metaphorical. For example, it made all the difference by affecting choices of meaning and tone while translating "It Was the Pulse Flying," to learn from the poet that it was not a poem "about" ecstatic religious experience, using metaphors of flight, fever, rising, and falling, but a poet-grandmother describing a loved grandchild dying from fever. Similarly, it made all the difference in translating a number of poems filled with images of light, lamps, flames, fires and darkness (as in "When the Hand of Darkness" and "You Leave, I'll Stay") to learn from the poet that these were neither archetypal symbols of a Persian version of the fire-bird story (a monster's hand reaching down from the clouds to pick a "pear of light") or conventional metaphors for freedom and oppression ("flower of light" "hiding," "choked in a lamp") but poetic recollections of a horrifying historical experience: nights of blackouts and mass executions during the War with Iraq. It made all the difference to know when a cigar was a cigar or something else in these poems; the act of clarifying almost always added to their charge of meanings and feelings.

There are others too who have helped the translators on both sides of the linguistic and cultural divide: Shahla Haeri, Abbas Milani, Shawali Ahmadi, and Sadr-ed Din Elahi in discussing different interpretations of the poems in Persian; Michele Safa in the idiomatic fine tuning of these poems in their second language; Paul Friedrich and Michael Beard reading early versions of the translations and offering useful advice; Rena and Jack Franklin, Lynn Franklin and Robert Sweeney, and Marsha and Tom Collins, patiently reading various drafts of these translations and commenting on the idiom, grammar, potential interpretations, and beauty of the poems. To all these people the translators owe thanks.

We Await the Golden Dawn

૭

Simin Behbahani

I have returned from buying groceries. Bringing the bags of fruit and fresh vegetables from the car to the elevator is hard for me. I feel I no longer have the agility or strength of days gone by. I tire easily. Sometimes, I feel shooting pains in my knees. But, then, that's life, and its passage exacts an inevitable toll. Every time I reveal my aches and pains to my friends, even if I do it rarely, they say, they are "accidents of your birth certificate." Then they say, "I am in relatively good health." It may be so. Perhaps I owe this good health to the milk of that village wet-nurse who had two white, soft, warm udders instead of breasts and nurtured me abundantly from those fountains of sweetness.

Really, what do I remember from that time? Almost nothing, except a few hazy images. This one for example: I am in a garden and I have found a piece of charcoal. I put it in my mouth. It tastes flat, tasteless, just like some moments in life. Or this one: I have picked up my nanny's prayer stone from her prayer rug, and am chewing it with my freshly sprouted teeth, unmindful of her severely enunciated *Allahu Akbar*(s). Most children try out the taste of dirt. Isn't this what is meant by the saying, "ultimately we turn into clay for the potters?" Isn't the child's mouth only testing the taste of the dust that will cover it eventually?

I also remember the kindergarten run by some American missionaries: my dancing at the end-of-the-school-year celebrations, as a yellow flower, wearing a yellow, organdy skirt, full of ruffles. And why yellow, since I preferred the red dress of my friend, who was playing a red rose? Even the

This essay was first published in *Nimeye Digar* 2, no. 1 (1993): 169–76.

poem she recited was rhythmically richer than mine: "I am a red rose, the king of all the flowers, all the flowers, all the flowers." In comparison, I had to recite: "I am a yellow rose, the Sultan of all the flowers, the Sultan of all the flowers." And no matter how I tried to quicken or slow down the rhythm of my words, they would not rhyme. Even at that age, only two or three years old, I had enough metrical sense to abbreviate Sultan and say, "I am a yellow rose, the 'tan of all the flowers, the 'tan of the flowers." I don't remember any more how I finally came to terms with that Sultan. (My son has written on the margin of the rough draft of this essay: "You have never come to terms with any Sultan.")

I have always liked the color red, perhaps because of that yellow costume alongside that badly metered poem and my friend's red costume and her well-metered poem at that school celebration. That envy and passion for red have stayed with me to this day. Before the wedding with my first husband, I went out shopping with him, and everything I bought was red: red shoes, red purse, red blouse, red jacket . . . And when my father saw all that red, he frowned, "You think you are a peasant bride?"

Maybe my writing about these things is an unconscious attempt to evade mentioning my birth date. How can that be? A biography certainly needs this date. All right then, if it needs to be written, it should be written: Simin Behbahani, 1927– . I only hope the blank space will be filled while I still possess a working body and productive mind. One of my worries is to experience life and helplessness at the same time. May it not be so.

I was not born yet when my father, Abbas Khalili, and my mother, Fakhri Arghun, began drifting apart. By the time I was two, a little after my grandfather's death, their separation became official. I was three when my mother remarried. My father did not remain unmarried either. I have probably inherited my literary talents from both my parents. My father was the author of dozens of novels and scholarly and historical books. He was among the first Iranians to begin writing fiction in a western style. *Dark Days, Secrets of the Night, The Temple of Sam'an* are among his novels. *The History of Cyrus* in two volumes is his book of research. *The Light of Islam* in two volumes and *The Complete History of Ibn Athir* in fourteen volumes are works he translated. Copies of the widely read newspaper *Eghdam*, edited by him before the Pahlavi regime and again for twenty years after September 1941, can be found in the National Library of the Majlis and in other reputable libraries. His provocative and sharply written editorials are still remembered by many of his now-aged countrymen.

My mother, I believe, was among the wonders of her day. In an era when reading and writing were considered sinful for women, she came to benefit from many of the fields of learning available to her. She learned Persian literature, Islamic jurisprudence, Arabic, astronomy, philosophy, logic, history, and geography under the tutelage of recognized masters who also taught her two brothers. From childhood she studied French under a Swiss governess at home. My mother was fortunate to be raised in the bosom of a mother and a father who were, in the expression of the day, "enlightened," as well as affluent, and who would not miss any opportunity in educating their children. Not everyone enjoyed such a blessing.

My mother used to say that when her father was taking his leave of this world, not much of his wealth remained, but he had bequeathed his children a capital they would never lose: the learning he had provided them at great expense.

After her father's death and her separation from her husband, my mother began teaching French at the two existing girls' schools, Dar-ol Muʾallemat and Namus. She wrote poetry and stories, had a working knowledge of music and could play the tar well. Early in her youth she founded with several other women intellectuals the Society for Patriotic Women. For many years she and her associates would continue their efforts to teach and inform their fellow countrywomen.

I grew up in an environment never empty of poetry, enthusiasm, and action. From the age of twelve I could string together a few verses. At fourteen, I wrote a few poems which I recited at school. My teacher encouraged me. My mother sent my first ghazal to the journal *Now Bahar*, published by Malek-ol Shoʾara-ye Bahar with assistance from his son-in-law, Yazdanbakhsh-e Qahremani. My ghazal was accepted and published. It began with the lines: "O moaning starving masses, what will you do? / O poor anguished nation, what will you do?" I was no more than fourteen years old. It was an appropriate poem for an experimenting and talented youth.

I almost completed the six years of secondary school in four by taking two classes each year. However, before getting my diploma, I enrolled in the school for midwifery. The school authorities knew about my activities in the youth organization of the Tudeh party. They also knew that I occasionally wrote, including poetry. I had just begun my second year when a critical report about the undesirable conditions at the college was written anonymously in one of the newspapers of the day. The report enraged the president of the college; and I was accused of writing it, even though, to this day I don't know who wrote it. With four other classmates, I was summoned to the president's office. Without any preliminaries, College President Dr. Jahanshah Saleh directed at me a barrage of curses and insults. I answered back, reminding him that he had no right to insult any students this way. He responded by immediately slapping me in the ears and face. Quickly, I returned the slaps. We were practically at each other's throats, teacher and student. The vice-president of the college and other doctors intervened. They separated us and put an end to this scandalous event. I had responded to his injustice. But what comparison: his heavy, male hands, and my slight girlish hands? In a few minutes, my face and around my eyes were black and swollen.

My family filed a complaint in the courts. The Tudeh party created an uproar in my defense, and the newspapers had found something to write about. The president of the college expelled me and the four other students. For a couple of months the Tudeh party continued its campaign to have us readmitted to the college. It even organized a few street "meetings" or demonstrations in our support. Then, all of a sudden, it became silent and ordered us to compromise and keep quiet. Recently, years after the incident, I heard from one of the old Tudeh party leaders, now bearing their scars in voluntary isolation, that the leadership of the party had decided to withdraw their support of the expelled students for fear of jeopardizing the positions of three ministers the party had in the cabinet. My four friends, who were not as deeply involved in the events as I was, gave in. They returned to school. However, as hard as I tried, I could not accept the humiliation, admit a sin I had not committed, nor would I barter my freedom for the benefits of continuing my education or something like this. I quit my studies, and so changed drastically the face of my destiny.

From that time, the purpose of my poetry has been to fight injustice. Whenever I could, I have portrayed it, revealed it. I have considered freedom the cardinal requirement of being a poet, and have never bowed my head to any power or office.

After my expulsion from the college, I decided to marry the first person who would ask for my hand. And thus, in a couple of months, I married Mr. Hassan Behbahani. I was seventeen years old and beaten by forces stronger than me. I had surrendered myself to fate. During the wedding ceremony, I realized my tears were, drop by drop, washing off my makeup and running on my neck, wetting my white blouse. I would shed more such tears later, when in the middle of many nights I would be sitting awake in bed as my husband slept soundly by my side. Why? I did not know exactly. My heart was agitated, troubled. It was as if my body had taken on the smell of camphor. From my vantage point everything appeared dark. I had fled the fires of hell only to find myself in a frigid wasteland that would not reduce me to ashes but make my wandering hopes learn of a perpetual ice age. I could see no other image but a sterile land covered in cruel snow.

I should not be unjust, for poetic sake. My husband came from a respectable family. He had a relatively adequate education. He was a high school English teacher. But our temperaments were incompatible. Our outlooks on life were completely different. Yet, he did not stop my poetry. He did not prevent me from continuing my education. In his house, I recovered my faith in life and my ability to struggle. I finished high school. I took the entrance exams in a number of colleges and was admitted to the law school. I came to have three children by him. I lived with him for twenty years, though without any contentment, even for a day or an hour. I was able to get used to him and help him in his sickness and suffering. But my heart, this iron fortress, remained closed to him. We were two partners, trapped and unfulfilled, forced to live in harmony with each other. Eventually, our incompatibilities became overwhelming. We left the courtroom calmly and silently and went our separate ways. However our life had been together, it had blessed us with three children.

I chose another husband, Manouchehr Koushiyar. It is now eight years and a few days since I lost this second husband, whom I loved very much. I was at his side for fourteen years. Suddenly, that man, my companion of the road, died of a heart attack, entrusting me to loneliness. But, then, what is there to do, it was fate. I had met him when I was studying at the law school. Years later, I realized the bonds of this simple and honest relationship were permanent for me. Do they hold me, even now?

We finished Law School together. I became a high school literature teacher, and in that profession I remained. He did various kinds of legal work. In short, happy were those days spent with the beloved. As for the rest?

I finished my formal education in law, with criminal justice as a specialty. Yet all my life I have not stopped studying, including studying law. In fact, I still can, within certain limits, present an informed opinion on legal issues. My eldest son, ʿAli, is my best helpmate in reading and learning new things. He keeps me up to date with literary events. The books I don't have the patience to find, he makes available to me. And when I don't have the patience to read some of them, he offers me a selection of their important points. He is the first audience for my new writings. I always value his judgment and frequently realize he is correct. He is a good translator in his own right. He has translated a biography of Chekhov, which is now in the process of being published.

I have traveled to most places in Iran and seen my countrymen in their various ways of life, temperaments, and appearance. I have memories of all sorts of people, places and things: of the fine tiles of Isfahan; the massive ruins of Baam fortress; the sun setting behind still palm trees in the South; the tombs of Saʾdi, Hafez, Khayyam, Ferdowsi, Baba Taher, and Avicenna; the valley of Morad Beyg; the Heyran pass; the Caspian Sea and Lake Rezaiyeh; the rivers Karun and Aras. I also have memories of bombs, the hail of rockets, and wars, of September 1941 and October 1980, and of peace, revolution, mourning, weeping . . . O, O my country, with your past, your poets, your rulers, your endurance, and all that you have suffered, and, your triumphs: your winter's end . . .

I have also traveled many times outside of Iran, although only to a few places. I have been to America and England four times, and once each to France and Germany. Every time I have left Iran I have spent the nights thinking about the date of my return and the mornings counting the remaining days till my return. To no other land have I given my heart but Iran. It is as if this verse has risen from the depth of my soul: "Here were all my joys, poems, and passions. / Here is my throne, coffin, and tomb."

I hope my final resting place will be at the shrine of Emamzadeh Taher, close to where my husband and grandchild are buried and a few artists.

During my last trip to America (fall of 1990 and winter of 1991), I covered a lot of territory. I recited poems, lectured, and answered questions at eleven universities and cultural centers. I felt extremely close to my compatriots living outside Iran. People would come to hear me with hearts pining for their country. I realized how much I love my people, whether they lived in Iran or outside. Even though I had not planned it that way, I felt the language of my poems to be the language of the people. I felt I know what they want, and they understand what I say. That is enough for me.

Here is what I have published so far:

1951 *The Broken Setar,* poems and two short stories
1956 *Footprints*
1957 *Candelabrum*
1963 *Marble,* the fourth printing of this collection replaces the forced
    deletions with nineteen additional ghazals
1973 *Resurrection*
1981 *A Trajectory of Speed and Fire*
1983 *Plains of Arzhan*
1989 *Selected Poems,* distributed in 1991
1989 *On Art and Literature,* conversations with Naser Hariri, and an
    interview with the poet, Hamid Mossadeq
1990 *That Man, My Male Companion of the Road.*

This list includes all my work through 1990. From then on, I have published occasionally in a few periodicals of my choice. A collection of my new poems entitled *Clothes Like Paper,* which includes poems up to 1990, has recently been published in America by Zamaneh Publications.[1] I have also

---

1. Since 1992 Simin Behbahani has published *The Gypsy, the Letter, and Love* (1994); *Sing More Lovingly Than Ever* (1994); and *A Window to Freedom* (1995).

lately published another collection with ʿElmi Publishers. A collection of articles, interviews, critical analysis, and personal views is also ready for print but I don't know when it will be published. There are also a few short stories that I should add to the list.[2]

I have worked mainly in the ghazal style. I began writing poems with ghazals and linked couplets. From early on, my poems have reflected my social milieu and conditions, though in effect, these reflections have been reflections of my individual and emotional reactions to the society and conditions in which I have lived. I have never ignored inner, individual, and private feelings. I have never set out deliberately to write socially or politically engaged poems. Yet, often without intending to or being aware of it, my poems have been very much engaged in this way. Reacting to and provoked by the outside world, I reveal the world within.

For the past twenty years, I have tried to change the current meters of the ghazal by incorporating parts of natural, everyday speech, which in their natural setting may seem devoid of any obvious metrical design. By repeating and extending the meters of a beginning segment, I create a new pattern, free of the set patterns in traditional ghazals and free of the set themes and expressions associated with them. Thus, I have created a new container ready for new contents, while, at the same time, keeping the overall geometric shape of the conventional ghazal. This innovation opens so many possibilities that I can create a fresh metrical design for every fresh ghazal based on the meters of the first phrase that comes to my mind. Of course, I do repeat some of the meters because they have become familiar in my mind. I may repeat them automatically and unconsciously, a repetition which may also habituate the ears of their listeners.

Today I see younger poets following this form in their composition of ghazals. I do not believe in imitation, nor do I claim my innovations to be the only way for the ghazal to survive. But it is heartwarming to me to find some of the younger poets accepting this style. It justifies for me some of the judgments I have made in my work. Be that as it may, I have said things in this style that were neither customary or possible to say in the traditional ghazal.

I wish I had tried more. But this is as much as I could, given the constraints of jobs and making a living [outside literary work], a condition shared by many of my colleagues. Unfortunately, at this time and in our society, poets and writers have only their leisure time to spend on artistic and literary work, the rest they must work on earning a living.

---

2. *What Did I Buy with My Heart?* (1996).

By the way, I have also translated a pamphlet from the "What Do I Know?" series, on modern French poets, compiled by Pierre de Boidefer. While working on it, I came to realize how my compatriot poets have been striving shoulder-to-shoulder with contemporary poets elsewhere for poetic innovation and for keeping poetry alive; yet, they have been too humble to make their voices heard beyond their borders. Or perhaps it is our language that cannot appeal to a more worldwide audience. Clearly a poem in French or in English is many times more likely to be translated into various languages than any poem in Persian. Our writers and poets clearly lose out in this respect.

In any event, if we cannot do more, it is for us to do our best within our limits. It is a responsibility we cannot refuse or deny. May the future be in our favor. Hoping for a better day, we take steps towards our convictions. Darkness will roll back. The light will spread like silver. We await a golden dawn.

Simin Behbahani
Teheran, Iran
July 19, 1992

An Interrupted Speech (Untitled)

Dear Ones, Friends, Compatriots:
I am here today, purely on my own, without the advice or approval of my fellow writers, to voice concerns I have not been able to express publicly for the last twenty years.

Today, we are told, is National Reconciliation Day. May it be blessed. My fellow writers and I have never been estranged from anyone. But there has been a group, a political faction, that has allowed itself to inflict on us all kinds of insults, humiliations, and injuries. Of course, such treatment cannot stop writers and thinkers, as particles of dust cannot fill the skirt of heaven.

With the Revolution victorious, we thought freedom would now spread its wings over all our heads. Alas, from the very beginning, we witnessed things that we should not have seen and did not deserve to witness.

I remember the day when the documents and the tapes of the Writers' Association were pillaged, piled like rubbish on the ground. Some writers were arrested for their political views. Some, like Saʾid Soltanpour, were executed.

Some, fearing persecution, left the country and are to this day living with the hardships of life in exile. No effort has been made to bring them back. Some have died in foreign lands, with the sadness of exile, with the sadness of separation from their homeland and from an audience. When we held a memorial service for the prominent author and playwright, Gholam Hos-

On October 23, 1997, "The National Reconciliation Day," the Ministry of Culture and Islamic Guidance organized a festival to celebrate Woman's Day and National Reconciliation. Simin Behbahani was among the invited participants. Her speech, however, was interrupted a few minutes after she took the podium. She was not allowed to finish her talk. The full text of her presentation was published later in several journals outside Iran, including *Rouzegar-e Now* 16, no. 9 (Oct.–Nov. 1997): 52–56 [trans.].

sein Sa'edi, our opponents called us, in their widely circulated newspapers, "the dead risen from the grave." They attacked us with all kinds of moral, sexual, ethical, political, and religious slanders.

Those of us who stayed in the country have had to struggle with oblivion, with censorship, with the banning of our books and our names, with the violation of our civil and human rights, with poverty and unemployment and with financial and psychological pressures. Our only consolation is the two meters of our homeland that will be used for our eternal resting place when we die.

Some have been crushed by the hardships and died before their time. Such was Mehdi Akhavan Sales, who could have enriched his country's literary heritage for many more years. Others could not survive imprisonment. Such was Sa'idi Sirjani who walked into captivity with his own two feet and left in a coffin. Others died in mysterious circumstances with no effort made to shed light on the cause of their deaths. Such were Ahmad Mir'Alai, Dr. Ahmad Taffasoli, Ghafar Hosseini, and Ebrahim Zalzadeh. Some committed suicide, like Ghazaleh 'Alizadeh, inside the country, and Eslam Kazemiyeh, in exile within France.

> The pupil of my eye is soaked in blood
> Where do they inflict such tyranny on men?[1]

What had we done to deserve such spiritual and material annihilation?

When some compatriots of ours see us in the streets, they find it difficult to recognize us. "Are you still here?" they ask, eliciting a response such as "Where else should we be?" What they really mean, but are too shy to ask, is: "Are you still alive?"

Those of us who stayed in the country, putting up with all the hardships, have on occasion mingled our voices with the voices of our compatriots outside the country. On occasion, we have gone to visit them, conveyed a greeting or a message, and returned. Once, one such compatriot, showing enthusiasm for my visit and my poems, asked: "Why go back? Stay here." I replied, "My cries have reached your ears from inside the country. I will go back to the same place to call out to you, 'come back.'"

Now, scarred by years of suffering, by debilitating diseases and successive surgeries, by pressures of censorship and insults and threats to my freedom, I find my powers depleted and at their end. I think it has been for the best that my fellow writers outside Iran have stayed where they are and continue to work there.

---

1. Shams-ol-Din Mohammed Hafez, *Divan*, annotated by Parviz Natel Khanlari (Teheran: Kharazmi, 1980), 400 [trans.].

An Interrupted Speech

Now a new government has undertaken—or, in reality, has been commissioned by the people—to perform a very difficult task, the accomplishment of which requires true devotion.

> If you travel the desert desiring Kaaba
> Don't fret if taunted by the thorn-bush.[2]

Fear is useless. It is necessary to take on difficulties and obstacles, even at the cost of one's life. I agree with Galileo when he said "Unfortunate is the nation that needs a hero."[3] Yet, it has always been such national heroes that have given us the reason to hope for salvation. An effort must be made, because time is running out fast.

> The path to Layli's house is filled with obstacles
> To take it, the first requirement is to be Majnun.[4]

Simin Behbahani

Teheran, Iran

October 23, 1997

---

2. Ibid., 250.

3. Presumably, the poet is referring to the words of Galileo in Bertolt Brecht's play, *Life of Galileo* (translated by Charles Laughton and John Willett (New York: Arcade, 1994, 98, 153, 253–54), responding to the denunciations of a disillusioned disciple, and to Andrea Sarti calling Galileo a "wine-pump" and "snail eater" for refusing the role of the savior-sacrificial-hero (for "officially" taking back his revolutionary ideas in order to save his neck and get on with his life and work) and bemoaning, "Unhappy the land that has no heroes!" The quotation from Brecht/Galileo, without necessarily a sense of its context in the play, has enjoyed currency among many Iranians in their talk about heroes and revolutions. Thus we can find in the heady days just before the fall of the previous regime an angry article by Esma'il Jamshidi in the magazine *Ferdowsi* (Monday, Aban, 1357 [1978], 19) addressed to Brecht: "Mr. Brecht! Begging your pardon, I have something to tell you: Have you heard of Jalal Al-e Ahmad and Qolam Reza Takhti?" [Iranian heroes maligned by the Brecht quotation, making Brecht out to be a "qahreman-kosh" (hero-killer)].

4. Hafez, *Divan*, 914. For readers unfamiliar with the figure from Middle Eastern/Persian literature and folklore, Majnun embodies the selfless, self-sacrificing lover, forsaking all (family, power, privilege, human society, physical comforts) for the sake of love, becoming in the process an archetypal figure for the poet, madman, and hermit.

The Poems

His Master's Voice

This antique lacquered disk,
where is the tool to make it sing?
With the dog and megaphone on its label,
it's a pity if it remains silent.
Tell this dog sitting on its haunches
to bark with all its might:
to awaken, perhaps, from their sweet sleep
the faithful Companions of the Cave.*
Their old coins have become our oft-told tales.
The enchantment of our childish hearts
cannot be purchased with current coinage.
The heart of childhood beats
with childish rhythms.
Malign it not by calling it sick.
No doctor knows its secrets.

Speak, ancient record, speak!
Where's that woman, master of the house,
to wipe off the dust from your face
and the sorrow from your heart?
Where is she, to crank the handle with her soft hands
and make the needle of my childhood years
run in the grooves?
Where is she, to let the little girl decked in silk and lace
twirl like a bouquet of flowers,
dancing to your music?

From *A Window to Freedom*, 1995 [1994], 161–63. The title of the original Persian poem is in English, in Latin script [trans.]. The order of the poems in this edition reflects their time of publication, beginning with the most recent. The first date represents the publication date of its original collection, and the date in brackets refers to the year the poem was written, when available.

*From a Rip van Winkle–like story, referred to in the Qoran (Sura 17, "The Cave") and elaborated in legend and folklore. It is about seven men and a dog, who took refuge in a cave, and went to sleep for several hundred years. When they woke up, they tried to buy some food, not realizing their coins were no longer current [author and trans.].

The crank and my mother's soft hands
are both lost.
In the disk's grooves
the needle can no longer gallop.

O broken, lacquered disk,
where are Taj, Adib, and Qamar?
What happened to Morteza,[†]
who could set the *tar*'s pulse
flying with his pick?

They are all asleep,
and, sadly, sleeping persons cannot sing.
The cries of owls and ravens have torn our tired ears.
Time has changed its countenance.
The passions of childhood have come to an end.
The lacquered disk: it is better if it remain silent.

----

†Four well-known musicians from the time of the poet's childhood [trans.].

A Thousand Golden Butterflies

A thousand golden butterflies flutter among the lilies.
A thousand lanterns light the hall of mirrors.
From the horizon a woman approaches,
wearing a robe of silk and flames,
carrying a thousand fresh oranges in her arms and skirt
and a thousand more on a silver and crystal tray,
balanced coquettishly on her head,
as if proclaiming: look, it's all mine.
A thousand fresh oranges roll down,
each dispersing its inner light at her feet.

From the desert a woman approaches,
wearing a robe of salt and wounds,
her ears still filled with the ravens' cries,
in her head swirling a thousand enraged bees,
her body bound by a thousand iron chains,
her kindness a secret even to the doves,
though there is room in her heart
for more than a fistful of grains.

You arrive from a land far away,
dawn's herald of love and rapture,
your heart a hall of mirrors,
your eyes a garden of lilies.

The woman coming from the desert
now rests on the horizon,
the rising of her orange heart
spreading its radiance on the fields and the valleys.
Free of the terrors of the desert,
she wears a dress of silk and kisses
and a splendorous golden crown.

From A Window to Freedom, 1995 [1993], 119–21.

A thousand golden butterflies
dance ecstatically in her head.
For this is the morning, the beginning of light.
For this is love, the season for things to grow.

Oh, I Made Love!

Oh, I made love—to what kind of a beast?
In what nightmare? In what hallucination?

There was sleep, there was wakefulness.
There was desire, there was repulsion,
in conflict and union, like a hand grasping a collar.
There was love, there was hate,
there was pleasure, there was loathing,
like being with a beautiful gazelle,
dead in the desert.
Oh, I want to vomit:
how could I drink in my drunkenness
the polluted water in that crystal cup.
I must endure the flames to purify the pollution.
I must throw myself in a burning oven.

I wish I could turn into a snake.
I wish I could shed my skin,
then flee from my self in a shining body.
But, no, I am a rusty sword,
naked, without a scabbard,
I flee, but my body runs with me.
The body is mine, but I am a fugitive,
tired of my body.

Oh, I made love. I found it a coin with two faces:
Gabriel's image on the front,
and a demon's image on the back.

From *A Window to Freedom*, 1995 [1992], 111–12.

The Child Trailed Behind

The child trailed behind, whining: I want pistachios!
The woman sighed: where shall I get the money?
The child ran into the store, braying like a donkey,
stamping his feet.
The owner pulled him by the ears, demanding:
where's your owner, little beast?
The mother pulled the child by the arm:
see, what shame you've brought us?
The child, with or without understanding,
shook his head.

It boggles the mind, she was thinking:
the prices for a drink and an ice cream,
a hundred *tomans* for a few pistachios!
Weary of her life of drudgery,
she was thinking of her son's renunciations:
the fresh walnuts he had forsaken yesterday,
the fresh renunciations everyday,
added to the old ones.

The child trailed behind.
The woman gazed at him with eyes in which anger
had been washed away by a rain of tears.
She suddenly noticed his bulging pockets.
Oh, no, she cried. You stole them?
The child was smiling a pistachio-smile,
his mouth full of pistachios.

From *A Window to Freedom*, 1995 [1993], 165–66.

I Gave My Face to the Scalpel

I gave my face to the scalpel,
to make it young perhaps,
to make it an object of admiration
in the eyes of everyone.
The heart with a pretty face thirty years ago
wants the same now in its old age.
I told it, I cannot suffer such wounds.
Why should I hide it: it makes me fear
for my very life.
It answered, what young face
is not worth life itself?
As precious as life may be,
I would throw it in the fire
for such a face.

The scalpel made my face young again,
but sadly my heart stayed the same.
If the scalpel could have changed it too,
I would have offered it my heart.
What had taken over my despondent heart
To wish to change to water when it was ice?
To change to a lion from a decrepit cat?
Oh, with what words can I tame it?
To what sorcerer can I go to transform with a spell
the pathetic cat into a mighty lion?

From *A Window to Freedom*, 1995 [1992], 109–10.

I Am So Full of Light

I am warm. I am happy, a luminous candle.
My soul is in flames. It is rising from my body.
How sweet it is! How grateful I am!
Our separation has ended:
this is you and this is me, together!
Be my Spring: cover with flowers
my arms and lap like the branches of a tree.
If clothes come between us
I will discard them.
Happy is a blushing face:
in its burning coals I will incinerate
dark shame.
My heart turns to water,
though I am made of fire.
My body has turned to wax,
though iron is what I am.
I fly every dawn like a dove
in the ambience of love.
Desiring you, I disperse the particles of my soul
like a flower's perfume.
I perform the part of the dancing flame.
I am so happy. I am so full of light.

From *A Window to Freedom*, 1995 [1992], 107–8.

I'm an Old Sanctuary

I'm an old sanctuary.
What fear do I have of getting old?
There are wines of a hundred kinds in my old tavern.
Inside me love has bloomed in such secret abundance
that it is whispered about by every breeze.
The white strands you see on the top of the cross
are silver dust fortune has sprinkled
from a winter cloud.

Every tired traveler seeking shelter
from the dust of the road
has been some time my guest and companion.
The displaced and the destitute have sat at my table
to share if only my crust of bread.
And if a thief stole some silver from my refuge,
my unbounded charity would guide him
to the right path.*
He who said "this is my blood, drink it!"
spoke the truth.
That is why such vines have grown in abundance
in my sanctuary.

From *From A Window to Freedom*, 1995 [1992], 97–99.

*These lines draw on Victor Hugo's *Les Miserables:* the spiritual turnaround of Jean Valjean by Bishop Digne's act of overwhelming and unexpected generosity. The embittered outcast had repaid the priest's original hospitality and kindness by stealing some silver. When caught by the police, the priest not only lied to save Jean Valjean but even added two silver candlesticks to the things he had stolen. A transformed Jean would repay others in need for the rest of his life [author and trans.].

The sorrow of the last supper
has been mixed in the mud of my being.
The olives of my Jerusalem are bitter
from the betrayal.
Only two half-loaves remain
from my years of striving:
take them both, I can't divide them.
Man or woman, bearing old wounds,
don't be afraid to let your head rest
on my compassionate breast.

I am down to the last string on my old lyre.
I pluck it in this last song to my heart's desire.

Has the Game Ended?

Has the game ended?
No, no, I don't believe it.
My heart cries like a naughty child: once more.
Did it pass by so softly because it feared
its too invigorating breeze would pull apart
a wilted flower?
Will my breast, that well-tuned instrument
stop playing the song it has played over twenty years
of your love?

I thought I could make your memories fade.
But I see traces of you everywhere,
on every nook and cranny.
It's as if the branches are dancing with love,
witnessing that first kiss.
There were days when this swing,
this intimate of my flowing skirt and hair,
was to us bed and cradle.
We were like two *kingfishes* in this pool,
companions in swimming and of the heart,
taking pleasure in our closeness.
If you ask the curtains about those hidden pleasures,
they will tell you of bodies dancing
crimson in the light.

To whom shall I talk of this pain,
of my beloved fleeing my embrace for another
because he could not find in this time-plundered garden
someone worthy of love?

Has love ended? Yes. It has.
Heart, death has come, even if you don't believe it . . .

From *A Window to Freedom*, 1995 [1992], 101–3.

13

A State Beyond Words

I am in a state beyond words.
I am another Simin today.
It's as if the sun has never shined before on my head.
It's as if the sky and I have always been strangers.
But, today, under this dark blue sky,
I have wings and feathers,
I am the doves' flying companion.
It's as if I have never opened the gate
to the flower garden.
Such freshness, such bloom,
overwhelm my credulity.
Am I drunk? No,
I haven't touched a drop.
But my heart—this pine cone—is happy,
filled with life.

Death is not that far away.
Since I cannot do my heart's bidding
tomorrow, from the mud
I will serve it today.
I am the short-lived lily, friend,
seize the time.
If you are not at my side today,
what use will it be tomorrow,
when I wilt?
I am a shining grape-cluster,
delicious from head to toe.
You trample my head with abandon,
unaware that I am more pleasing
to the palate.

End this procrastination,
this land belongs to you,
this is your city and sovereign.

From *A Window to Freedom*, 1995 [1992], 201–2.

I wait for you, to lay my life at your feet.
O, kind one, your letters have come
to share my sorrows in your place,
each spreading before me a flowering meadow.
O skillful harpist, play in a different mode
for a different way.
This is the road to take, the way home.
This is all I have to say.

Whirl, Whirl, My Friend

Whirl, whirl, my friend! O God, don't let me fall.
It's a tornado, panting, whirling in this game.
Whirl, and I will whirl. Again and again! Don't stop!
Till I'm finished with this, you can't wear me out.
If you threaten me, I shall rise like a twister
and fill the sky with dust.

I come from the past, yearning for childhood,
wishing that you too were a child again.
I come, rushing, panting, sweating.
Where else can you find such a spirited steed,
as fast, as nimble as me?
I come from the land of music, on wings of ecstasy.
Who will accompany me in this song?
I come from the shores of the Blue Danube.
Play the three-beat melody I have composed.
I come from a wine with no other design
on its crystal cup than my poems.
I come from a star that turns on its axis.
Consider me your axis. Whirl, whirl, my friend.

Sing, dance, my playmate! I am overflowing with sparks.
The song you make will catch fire in this flame.

From *A Window to Freedom*, 1995 [1991], 91–92.

I Write, I Cross Out

I write, I cross out, to find what I've lost,
to find words for turbulent thoughts.
I scratch the back of my skull
with a finger like an ivory dowel
to untangle braid by braid the tangled yarn.
In my mind filled with dust
the colors of your face have faded.
I close my tired eyes to contemplate
what remains.

I wanted to remember you. You changed into a cloud
on the far side of the sea.
How can I picture you from this scattered vapor?
Is this the tired wind breathing
or the sound of your voice in the streets?
Who is this and what is he saying?
I wish to know, that I may prepare an answer.
What is this turbulence
below the surface of my consciousness?
I am not the foam that breathes
with joy in the waves of the sea.
Your memories flee, and I have no remedy.
I cannot fold them in piles
like clothes in a closet.

You have asked me, what do I want from you?
You should ask, what I wanted.
Desires have been drained from my heart
before I could desire.

From *A Window to Freedom*, 1995 [1991], 199–200.

If the Snake Is Domestic

If the snake is domestic,
I will give it shelter.
I will be fond of it still,
even if it does cruel things.

It slithered down the ceiling
with angry carnelian eyes
and a quick poisonous tongue,
and it coiled itself by my side.
People tell me, bring it salt:
as salt consumed will
make one beholden to its giver.
I will bring what is needed
from my poems: images like emeralds
formed in my lover's soul.
I shall lay them in front of it
and enumerate them, one by one.
Dazzled by the colors and light,
it will begin warming up to me.
It will move its head,
expecting me to scratch its back and neck.
Its fangs glistening like brass,
a snake intoxicated—
what need to destroy it?
Oh, this is a domestic snake.
You can't kill it in anger.
Even though it does cruel things,
I let it be.

From *A Window to Freedom*, 1995 [1986], 173–74.

The Perfume of Coffee and Thoughts of You

My day begins with the perfume of coffee and thoughts of you
scattering desire on moments of joy.
Wakefulness, bitter, warm, arousing
is a nectar I drink from the cup of your eyes.
Like the morning breeze rippling through fields of violets,
thoughts of you ripple through my memory at first light.
The mornings when my eyes opened to your presence beside me
were like a snow-covered valley being kissed by the sun.
Oh, I have a new tale for you, The Thousand and Second Tale.
Listen to me, because I am Scheherazade.
With my enchantments I have filled each vein
with the gold of a galaxy,
to offer the treasure-trove of my heart to love.
My eyes are dazzled by so much love and light,
beyond my endurance—oh, heavens, help me.
I thought I would bring light to this somber night
with a spark of love,
oh, the fire spreads, oh, it is consuming me.

I was the fireside gypsy who at the day's end
found herself enveloped in a swirling silk of fire.

From *A Window to Freedom*, 1995 [1991], 197–98.

Orange-tressed Sun

Orange-tressed sun, when will you rise?
When will you completely melt this dirty snow?

Tempest, with a frown on your brow, when will you destroy
this house of horror and its ghostly inhabitants?

Green-eyed sea, with seed from what union will you transform
the grains of sand in the shells into fine pearls?

Thick, rain cloud, in what pond, in which plain,
will you dance with the sliding circles of waves and bubbles?

Vine, here are pail and water and your hundred hands and ropes,
when will you fill these unripe grapes with pure nectar?

O sky, I wish to rest next to a kind friend,
when will you change the cradle of your rainbow to a bed?

O poor heart, when the guest arrives,
with what coins will you provide for their sweets and wine?

O dream-knight, you promise, but never come.
I am dying of this hesitation. When will you show more haste?

When you are with me, your eyes will frame a portrait
in which the image of this gypsy is an emblem of love.

From *A Window to Freedom*, 1995 [1990], 79–80.

Caduceus

The world's symbol of well-being is unwell,
its wings both hurt, its snakes shriveled,
a stick without distinction, without bloom or sprout.
Where are those powerful wings, those clever serpents?
Not a soft breeze caresses it in the morning.
The Spring rain spares it not a drop.
If no one will revive it with a drink of water,
may my eyes be its bountiful spring.

For Adam's descendants the world is ill,
as if its turbulent body has fallen apart.
It is blue: its sadness spreading in jasmine fields.
It mourns: its sighs sprouting fields of tulips.
Its brain is insane: obsessed with blood.
When will a physician show compassion
for its sorry state?
Hippocrates sleeps in his grave,
distant from his wisdom and resolve.
The world's symbol of well-being
lies by his side like a piece of kindling.

From *A Window to Freedom*, 1995 [1991], 147–48. The title in the original Persian poem is in the Latin alphabet [trans.].

Bring Me the Palette

Bring me the palette,
my beloved wants me green.
When he comes thus,
he will find me green
from brain to skin.
Make me a pond,
my beloved wants me cool:
what pleasure to wash this fire
from my soul.
What shall I say, if he doesn't care
for my washed out colors,
even if this dove
is as articulate as a parrot?
What can I do, if he can't stand
my self-immolation,
even if he knows he is the cause
of my conflagration?

O incredulous heart,
how quick is my pulse.
In my breast there is a turmoil again,
created by love.
Again my body is burning, hot.
Again my eyes are lit.
Again my heart is a garden.
Again this garden is paradise.

Love has come, I greet it.
It has come, defiant, and bold.
It has come with love-killing lateness,
the antidote.*

From *A Window to Freedom*, 1995 [1989], 59–60.

*Allusion to the antidote that came too late to Rostam, the epic hero from the Shah-nameh who unknowingly killed his son [trans.].

Kill me or burn me:
have I ever begrudged my life?
Whatever my friend commands
I will obey.

Footsteps

Who is passing through my street?
Whose footsteps are these?
Perhaps I should open the window.
Perhaps it's a messenger with news of love.
My heart is heavy from solitude.
Perhaps I should open the window,
if still in my quiet street
a passerby may pass through?

The one passing through carries flowers.
I can tell: the street has a different fragrance and hue.
The one passing through carries a torch.
Tell him: "tear this curtain of darkness
from this house of sorrow."

I am so wretched, so deprived:
tell him not to hold back.
The one passing through carries candies and rosewater.

See how it presses against my heart,
the leaden silence of the night.
His footsteps' silvery echoes signal the dawn.

Whose footsteps are these?
O heart, proclaim love!
The one passing through is looking at my window.

From *Clothes Like Paper*, 1992 [1989], 81–82.

Two Rows of Acacia Leaves

Two rows of acacia leaves: What balance! What order!
Such easy assembly! Such tranquil lining up.
As for me, I find no friends in congregations
and I feel restless in lines.
Without harmony or order: I am stubbornness personified.
I am the moss that spreads its dirt-entangled skirt in vain everywhere:
from marble breasts to backbones of clay.

Two rows of acacia leaves: What bright green letters!
Such terms! Such expressions!—in nature's book of poems.
As for my turbulent thoughts: no sentence can contain them,
as no cup can contain the dread and tumult of the sea.

Two rows of acacia leaves: All comrades! United! Single-hearted!
Companions so sincere! In such complete agreement!
Where is my accepting heart to serve as a refuge for patience?
My friendship is inconstant, my sympathy ephemeral.
I am not like the rising moon smiling in a mirror or water.
I am the heat and glitter of a scarlet dagger drawn from its sheath.
I have withdrawn from the world, wrapped my house in a curtain,
lest the sunshine penetrate my window a few feet.
I am far from the caravan's protection, like a solitary doe
driven by destiny and carelessness into a snare.
She should hold the stem of a row of acacia leaves like a rein
whose certainties do not fall apart under an attack of sadness.

From *A Window to Freedom*, 1995 [1989], 51–53.

Necklace

Anxious, agitated, sad,
her face uncovered, her head unveiled,
not afraid of arrest or policeman,
oblivious to the order, "Cover! Conceal!"
Her eyes two grapes plucked from their cluster,
squeezed by the times to fill a hundred barrels with blood,
mad, really mad, a stranger to herself and others,
oblivious to the world, beyond being awakened even by the deluge,
a particle of dust adrift in the wind, without purpose or destination,
lost, speechless, bewildered, a corpse without a grave,
carrying around her neck a necklace of curses and tears,
a pair of boots tied together belonging to a dead soldier.

I asked her: what does this mean?
She smiled: my son, poor child, sitting on my shoulders,
hasn't taken off his boots yet.

From *Clothes Like Paper*, 1992 [1988], 43–44.

Fossil

I am the trace of an unknown bird,
a fossil from eons past.
What flight is after such millennia
is beyond my comprehension.
I have seen the fine turquoise
beyond the branches above my head.
It fetches a high price in the market,
but my pockets are empty.
Every silver-breasted bird
crossing the blue sky like a meteor
mocks at my hopeless confinement
from its vantage of unfolding horizons.
If on a moonlit night a cloud
raises a mountain of cotton,
it will spare my broken-down nest
not a worthless piece.

I am the bird-like fossil, bound to this spot.
What else can move me from this confinement
but birds using me as a stepping stone?
Seeing two lovers with a single heart
touching beak to beak
draws sighs from my heart
like burning sparks.

Though bound to these stones,
I am still that melancholic bird.
How shall I fly towards you,
while I remain a lifeless fossil?

From *A Window to Freedom*, 1995 [1988], 259–60.

27

Our Tears Are Sweet

Our tears are sweet, our laughter venomous.
We're pleased when sad, and sad when pleased.
We wash one hand in blood, the other we wash the blood off.
We cry as we laugh at the futility of both these acts.
Eight years have passed, we haven't discovered their meaning.
We have been like children, beyond any account or accounting.
We have broken every stalk, like a wild wind in the garden.
We have picked clean the vine's candelabra.
And if we found a tree, still standing, defiantly,
we cut its branches, we pulled it by the roots.
We wished for a war, it brought us misery,
now repentant we wish for peace.
We pulled wings and heads from bodies,
now seeking a cure, we are busy grafting.

Will it come to life, will it fly,
the head we attach, the wing we stitch?

From *Clothes Like Paper*, 1992 [1987], 41–42.

I Sing in Your Voice

I sing in your voice in the blue skies of my beliefs
a song of flying inscribed by the wings of doves.

Wanting you I dance in a skirt of undulating sequins
like a pine forest dancing to a gentle breeze.

In your presence I see the green of my wings,
like the image of grass the feathers of a parrot paint in the mirror.

In the lines that define your being I seek a hedge
to protect the green clover from being trampled.

I grow in your consciousness like a vine,
with my hair covering rooftops, doorposts, and fences.

Your tongue burns me, I am the candle to your flame,
in your illumination my tears turn to precious gems.

With you in mind I build a castle as wide as freedom
in which high and low sit as equals.

I am the autumn's solitary pine, naked in the twilight,
with generous veins giving my blood to the marble.

From *Clothes Like Paper,* 1992 [1987], 79–80.

The Ants' Leftover

It is as if the brain in my skull were a split walnut
attacked by an army of strong, voracious ants.
It is as if my frenzied thoughts were red ants,
pillaging my brain, dragging their booty each way,
eating a piece here, dragging another for storage elsewhere,
leaving little for a scale to weigh.

It is as if the heart trembling in my breast were a candle
immolating itself: its wick dipped in blood,
its life draining away, shedding little light.

The road ahead is uneven,
its waters muddy, its flowers full of thorns,
beyond any shoe's endurance, beyond the strength of knees.

From a wrong suffered,
a scream smolders silently in my eyes,
like the cry of a doe from a hunter's arrow.

A flood of words, confused, meaningless, pour from my lips,
like bees' tumult in a burning hive.

Such is my condition: assailed
by sorrow as a falcon assails a sparrow
and by friends showering me with taunts
and reprimands, why do I not write the poems
expected of me?
I respond: I cannot imagine
my infirm brain producing anything better than this.
The best this ants' leftover can hope for
is a sweeping.

From *Clothes Like Paper*, 1992 [1987], 75–76.

A Man with a Missing Leg

A man with a missing leg
has one leg of his pants folded.
Anger burns in his eyes.
Is this a spectacle, they cry?
Though I turn my face away,
his image lingers in my eyes:
his extreme youth, less than twenty, perhaps.
I pray he will not be like me:
have to suffer another forty years.
Yet, the suffering that comes with existence
is impervious to such entreaties.
My feet were quick,
yet how difficult the path was for me.
How will he manage with just one leg?
Tap, tap, he stamps the pavement with his cane,
though he needs no signature
to register his presence.
My tender smiles turned to thorns and daggers in his eyes.
Used to rough treatment,
he has no appetite for tenderness.
Lines of bitterness mark his cold, parched face.
It's as if, with his body diminished,
his spirit too had lost its resilience.
To help him hang on, I thought, I would offer him
some kindness and motherly advice.
But I realized it was more than he could bear.

I turned to him to initiate a conversation.
The spot where he stood was empty.
He was gone, the man with a missing leg.

From *Clothes Like Paper*, 1992 [1987], 37–38. The historical setting of this poem is the war with Iraq, which produced over a half-million Iranian casualties. For an exegesis of this poem, see Karimi-Hakkak, in *Nimeye Digar* 2 (1993): 83–113 [trans.].

It's the End of the Line

It's the end of the line, and still you sit,
too tired, too broken down, to take another step.
O ancient flax, witness of my decline:
in my fingers you rot and fall apart.
You strain to live, but you are more tired
and broken down than you believe.

O heart, from you no desire can sprout.
You are a seed in the dead soil
of the dry desert of my body.
Wishing to fly, you can only utter an envious sigh.
Every breath you breathe is the air of confinement.
O yellow-faced autumn, with what colors or perfumes
do you wait to greet the happy birds?

Your battered rooftop deserves
no more than an ill-omened owl to make its nest.

They have turned to straw those twin braids
that were once like two bouquets of violets.

O spine, do not rebel against the burden of my body
while I have not escaped life,
while you have not escaped my body.

From *A Window to Freedom*, 1995 [1986], 39–40.

From the Street (6)

When the woman confessed for the fourth time,
stoning her to death became necessary
as commanded by religion.
The judge had opened this knot with his own hands:
revealing the hidden secret to the public.

The luminator of the laws
summoned the believers,
filling their breasts with light,
like the sun rising over the East.
One of them climbed a rooftop,
another climbed a tree,
and they made offerings of stones
and their strength on behalf of their faith.
But by and by they grew weary.
Their hands weakened,
their zeal waned.

There was still half-a-life
left in the woman.
Her guard, furious, enraged,
picked up a cement block
and brought it down hard on her head,
ending thus the unfinished business.

I thought, consider it a work
of benevolence by the unseen:
religion now falling in step with the times.
For this is the age of cement, not stone,
and, at last, death-by-stoning has given way
to death-by-the-cement block.

From *Clothes Like Paper*, 1992 [1986], 157–58.

33

A Lily, Like a Smoke Ring

A lily, like a smoke ring: dark, blue.

A cry from the river bank: whose? whose?
A cry from the extremities of sleep: arise! arise!
A scream from the roots of haste: hurry! hurry!

A lily, on the garden's skirt, a crimson flame,
toe to head, a contest of fire and smoke.
A garden, burning, abandoned by fortune and friends,
not a thread remains of that wondrous silk.
Flames and fur trees, twisting as they rise.
Crowns and stamens falling, falling.

A lily, yellow as death, cold as fear,
signs of death and fear on every petal.
With no hope left or spirit,
all flying is confined to a cage.
There are no songs on the lips,
but dirges.

A lily, like a black snake, coiled around the moon,
snatched it away, in its poisonous mouth.
No water flows from the Milky Way in the barren fields.
Stars, thirsty ewes, wander at the river's edge.

Plant a white lily with the face of the sun.
As it grows majestically towards heaven,
you will see light spreading across the plains,
you will see the day opening its pores to good fortune.

From *A Window to Freedom*, 1995 [1986], 247–49.

Heart, You Are So Restless

You are so restless, heart, calm down.
Wait for the flowering poppy,
for its mourning red to bear green fruit,
for its enduring yellow to teach you patience.
O cold, sad, heart, wait,
the happy gypsy will prepare the fire and smoke.
The very blade with which you slashed your veins
will in return infuse your veins with ecstasy.
May the sword of vengeance you have raised
against your friends descend instead
on the heart of the enemy.

O heart, small pond in the storm's path,
always cowering, the storm always on the attack,
O pregnant whore, all fear and surrender,
I will expose what you hide,
the pus-filled body you guard with such servility.
What is it but a corpse rotting
from head to toe?

O heart, in deep pain,
I consulted a physician last night.
For a cure he prescribed narcosis.
Wait, heart, wait,
for the poppy to grow.

From *A Window to Freedom*, 1995 [1986], 35–36.

The Windows Are Closed

The windows are closed. Love does not appear.
The eyes are awake. They have no power to see.
When lovers were aplenty, my heart had no stomach for love.
Now my heart is inclined. But lovers are scarce.
When my face was beautiful, there was no mirror.
There is a mirror now, but no beautiful face.
My black hair scorched many a victim.
Its remains are a pile of ashes, unwanted by anyone.
My army of faithful followers has left me,
those remaining have no fidelity.
Why have my willing captives lost their manners,
engaging only in my renunciation?
I thought I would sell them to someone else.
But shameless slaves have no value in the market.

O sorrow, plentiful, my companion, my friend,
stay with me, since in the house of my heart there is no other resident.
O mad heart, you have wasted a lifetime,
this sadness is your reward, even if you don't deserve it.
Don't look for the lost moment, for in the flowing stream
shapes repeat themselves but not their meaning.

I should stop this anguished talking.
You are sleeping. And one asleep has no ear for talk.

From *Clothes Like Paper*, 1992 [1986], 65–66.

You Won't Believe It

You won't believe it, I have stars in my fists.
When I squeeze them, patterns of light
seep out from every crevice,
and in my glass-like bones quicksilver glows green.
I have stars in my fists,
but I fear someone might steal them.
I stare at every corner.
I listen for every sound.
I see someone lurking in the dark:
a monster from the tales my nanny used to tell me,
his eyes volcanoes, spewing anger
like streams of violet and crimson lava.
It's him, I thought, the extortionist,
coveting in the darkness
the stars I hold so dear.

He attacked me. I screamed.
I realized, to win this fight I needed a weapon.
I threw at his head every rock I could get my hands on.
He fell, wounded, squirming in his own blood.

The monster has fallen from the heights to such dust.
But you won't believe it:
I have no more stars in my fists.

From *Clothes Like Paper*, 1992 [1985], 95–96.

In My Necessary Silence

Sweet bird, what do you sing about,
in my necessary silence?
Tell me without quibbling,
what do you know of the things I know?
Spread your wings and fly with joy,
since you are free.
Your flying may lighten the gloom
of the wing-tied captives.
In the cage of my breast
the birds of my words
have lost their feathers.
Their voices tremble with fear.

So much smoke, rust, and sorrow
fill my necessary silence,
that I have forgotten what is moonlight,
a garden or a feast.
In fear and salt marshes
poems and pomegranate blossoms rot,
while the bramble boasts like a drunk man.

Sweet bird, may your companions be
the dawn and the veil-rending sun.
I have clamped shut my mouth like an oyster,
hiding the light within.
Early Spring rains wash the dust
of flowers from your pollen-sprinkling wings.
Who will wash the dust of sorrows
from my memories?
Rain cannot wash the gloom
of rainy days.
Here there is no sun, no moon, or flicker of love.

From *A Window to Freedom*, 1995 [1985], 33–34.

Where is source of warmth here
or of light?
The bird flew with joy,
making circles after circles in the air,
delighting in the lightness of its wings.
I grew tired of my durability.

"I Swear on the Fig, I Swear on the Olive . . . "

I swear on the fig and the olive, the heavenly signs,
that the garden is burning with fever.
How terrible is such gardening.
I swear this on the fig and the olive, emblematic fruits,
one all sweet, the other all kind.
What use is sweetness in a forest where *halehel*,*
the monster, has appeared to poison life?
What has become of kindness
that the only branches you see are never caressed,
always shivering in fear of someone's wrath?
How can the gardener bear setting fire to the garden?
And I have not the leave to say, "stop it, if you can."
The bird that used to sing happy songs in the garden
now sings only dirges to the dust and ashes of flowers.
What has she done but sing songs of mourning
for her tender heart to become an arrow's target?

No figs remain or olives, only blood and mourning.
Never shall heaven fit inside this perpetual hell.
Not even a thorn will grow in this barren garden—
I swear on the fig and the olive, on everything that grows.

From *Clothes Like Paper*, 1992 [1985], 115–16. Qoran, Sura 95:1, "The Fig." The poem itself is untitled or titled simply as fifth in a series called "From an Intimation and a Passage" ("Az Esharati va Gozari") [trans.].

*Deadly venomous creature of legend and myth [trans.].

Glass-like Snow

"O you who are clothed!"*

What glass-like snow! What dreadful winter!
Love has withered and the fire has died
in my heart and bedroom.
What hard snow, unmelted by The Nowruz† sun,
unwashed from my soul.
You, who have wrapped a halo around yourself
like the moon,
turn your gaze at me one night:
I am naked like a star.
From what acts of kindness do I hope to spin
a cocoon to cover myself?
What sense of affection
can my fingers take to my heart
from the touch of another
like the charge from a piece of friction-warmed amber?
I have emptied the pitcher of my body:
it will not add to my amazement
if the newly arrived guest smashes it on the rocks.
Is it empty? No! No!
There is clear water in it, turned to ice,
water I cannot pour a single mouthful.
I used to wear a shawl of golden linen like the sun,
now I have nothing left but this rag.
Where in the night shall I hang this tattered robe
that makes nakedness more becoming?
I am as perplexed as that old man from Yush.‡

From *A Window to Freedom*, 1995 [1985], 263–64.
*Qoran, Sura 74:1 [trans.].
†First day of Spring, vernal equinox, Persian New Year [trans.].
‡Nima Yushij, poet (1895–1960), a founder of modernism in Persian poetry [trans.].

You, draped in velvet like a willow's flower,
look how I shiver, naked, like a dry willow.
I am another Damavand:§
how hard is the snow,
binding my body from head to toe.

---

§Cone-shaped mountain, northeast of Tehran, 18,934 feet high, dormant volcano, with permafrost, in which Zahak, the snake-shouldered king of Iranian myth and epics, is bound and imprisoned [trans.].

Twelve Fountains of Blood

"For what sin she was slain"*

On her shirt flowed the blood from twelve† fountains of blood.
In the dust of madness laid her twin jasmine braids.
Streams of blood ran down her body as if not from wounds.
Her mouth was open, as if an angel had made her smile.
It was as if her clothes were not sprinkled by a tyrant's lead,
but the sky had sprinkled stars in the cup of her body.
She who sat in my class, politely, for a year, has fallen.
She does not mind me anymore.
What would Ahriman want from an angel so pure?
His kiss and death have branded her breast,
even though the two buds there had not yet blossomed.
Who has the heart to surrender to a shroud
a body like porcelain, once accustomed to wearing silk?
Her presence will never again light up her father's eyes.
Brothers, what happened to her shirt in the thick of the night?‡

What was her sin? Tell me. It must be asked.
Don't keep it a secret, if you hear anything about it.

From *A Window to Freedom*, 1995 [1985], 265–66.

*Quotation from the Qoran, the apocalyptic Sura of Darkening (Sura 81:8, 9): "when the seas shall be boiling, / when the souls shall be coupled, / *when the buried infant shall be asked for what sin she was slain,* / when the scrolls shall be unrolled, / when heaven shall be stripped off, / when Hell shall be set blazing" (Arthur J. Arberry, trans. [New York: Macmillan, 1974]) [trans.].

†Twelve is the number of bullets in a clip used by semiautomatic guns used by the Iranian military at the time, here used to execute the poet's student [author and trans.].

‡Allusion to Qoranic/Biblical Joseph and to the bloody shirt which the jealous brothers brought back to Jacob as proof that Joseph (abandoned in a well) was killed by a wolf [trans.].

And Behold

"Do they not consider the camel, how it was created?"*

And behold the camel, how it was created:
not from mud and water,
but, as if, from patience and a mirage.
And you know how the mirage deceives the eyes.
And the mirage knows not the secret of your patience:
how you endure the thirst, the sand, and the salt marshes,
and gazing at the immense presence with your weary eyes.
And behold how this gaze is marked with salt grooves
like the dry lines remaining on your cheeks after a stream of tears.
And behold the tears that have drained from you
all means of consciousness.
With what nothingness should you fill this emptied space?
And behold in this emptied space the agitation of a thirsty camel,
made mad beyond the limits of its patience,
reluctant to carry meekly its heavy burden.
And behold its two incisors gleaming madly in a row of angry teeth.
Patience spawns hatred and hatred the fatal wound:
behold with what vengeance the camel
bit through the arteries of its driver.
The mirage lost its patience.
And behold the camel.

From *A Window to Freedom*, 1995 [1985], 267–68.
*Qoran, Sura 88:17 [trans.].

Raining Death

Spring, you are green again, why can't I see you?
You're visible and I have eyes, why can't I see you?

Spring, decked in flowers, wearing earrings of dew,
what has happened to my eyes that I cannot see you?

The violet's eyes and face, the blossom's perfumes and colors,
sadness engulfs me in a thousand folds, as I can't see them.

A thousand homes were destroyed, a thousand eyes wept,
Spring roll back your carpet of joy, as all I can see is mourning.

So many bombs have the planes poured down from the sky
that I cannot see any earth left in its place.

This is not hail falling, but seeds of death,
nothing else do I see but calamities falling from above.

The fires the two madmen set have turned two lands into wastelands,
I can see no justice in making the blood of people flow this way.

Except for thinking one day both men will die,
I can see no end to this predicament.

Spring, blood-scented, demented, tell me where is joy hidden?
On your branches I can only see death, no less abundant than the leaves.

From *Clothes Like Paper*, 1992 [1985], 35–36.

Thump, Thump, Thump, Echoed the Drum

Should we be raised,
when we are dead, dust, and bones?*

Thump, thump, thump,
the drum beat in the storm's jugular.
Line, line, line, zigzagged the cascading rain.
It was as if that atom-smasher was falling from God's throne:
particles exploding in space, with the laughter of demons.
The cobra raised and twisted its fiery body
like a sack of yellow arsenic thrown in fire.
Neither Noah remained or any living creature:
only I, alone, on an empty plain,
and the flood heading down the mountain,
seeking.

I thought I would flee:
but in their weakness my legs turned to vines,
disobeying every command.
I thought I would hang on to a tree:
but it turned to a blade,
shamelessly exposing my secret parts.
I ran my fingers through my hair:
each strand became a serpent.
It is but another ordeal, I thought,
this current carrying me,
smashing my head against the rocks,
scattering fragments of my eyes, lips and teeth.
Now here is my body, rubble without life or soul.
Tell my friends to make me rise again
from these ruins.

From *A Window to Freedom*, 1995 [1984], 269–70.
*Qoran, Sura 37:16.

Morse

Dash, dot, dot, dot, dash—
a songbird sings a song full of signs
from the branches of an elm tree.
As the night and the terror spread,
in my desperation to know,
the silences between sounds
convert every song into a message.
Perhaps from the borders of fire and blood,
perhaps from the fields of war and madness
a bird with a tired heart has brought a message
from a man with a tired body.
Her cries are daggers. Blood drips from her sighs.
Sadness chokes her like a noose.
Her moans question why these strife-smitten people
have drenched in blood the carpet of grass
spread by festive Zephyr.

Come, Paradise-lovers, this is Paradise,
with everywhere flowers sprouting
and jasmines in bloom.
You, heavenly heralds, why stoke the fires of hell,
set flame to people's lives and homes?

We are all parts of the same body,
similar in essence, told us that worldly-wise man.*
How will he face the mothers and their tears,
that iron-hearted pourer of molten lead
in the dead of night?

O songbird, I have listened to your secrets.
I know something must be done,
but not by someone with her hands tied like me.

From *Clothes Like Paper*, 1992 [1984], 89–90.
*Saʾdi (d. 1291) [trans.].

Dash, dot, dot, dot, dash—it's a message I misinterpret.
Silence, you won't break with this poem or that song.

When the Hand of Darkness

When the hand of darkness
picked that pear of light,
I imagined the night, this barren desert,
had lost its patience.
I saw the smoke descending
from the four directions
change into a black demon
and pick that luminous pear
hanging by its thin stem.
The wind made the window
open and shut its eyelids,
every time sending a wave
billowing through the curtains
and their fringes like lashes.
In the darkness I could see headlights
moving with the glint of blades,
striking fear in the heart
of the city infested by the night.
I could see my body lying in bed,
emptied, abandoned,
as if a snake had extracted itself
from my lifeless skin.

Once I adorned myself with stars
and played with mirrors and moonlight.
Of such a past and such a self
I could no longer find a trace.
From the rooftop came such a clamor,
as if a performing giant were banging together
two iron mountains.

I thought I would go to the garden
to let the night breezes clear the dark clouds
from my dim and tired mind.

From *Clothes Like Paper*, 1992 [1984], 87–89.

But what good is a garden
without sweet-singing ringdoves?
What good is a garden
filled with the moans and groans of an old crow?
What room is left
for the jasmine and lily to breathe
when the old ghosts and their deadly ways
ride the caravan of breezes?

I have seen such torrents of blood
carrying so many corpses,
that sleep has abandoned
the borders of my eyes.

Thorned Fruit

Thorned fruits, on the branches of the sycamore:
knots, opened by the caressing Spring.

Remember the days when Spring caresses
made me open the sadness of my heart to friends-in-sorrow.

Thorned fruits, brown, covered with spines:
miniature designs of my heart, tied to the branches.

Remember the days when the horseman arrived:
I was sitting with my back to the road, sulking at all horsemen.
He grasped me by the sleeves, and called me "my darling."
Of all my days those were the kindest.

Thorned fruits, murdered, and mute,
telling silently the story of the hanged.

What became of that horseman?
He left. I never saw him again.
It was July. My tears were like rain,
the color of blood.

The thorned fruits answer me,
with shriveled bodies from which had grown
a thousand spears . . .

From *A Window to Freedom*, 1995 [1984], 27–28.

From the Street (3)

— Tell me, what is given out here?
— Most likely, something worthwhile. Let's stop.
— Well, what is it?
— Whatever it is, it must have, for sure, some use.
— All this commotion!
You would think there is a flying elephant.
— Yes, no less impossible,
to pluck one hair from a bear
is nothing to scoff at these days.*

— A man is squeezing me.
— Ignore it. Say nothing.
He is teaching you how the pressure feels
inside the grave.

— My feet are freezing.
— Then, run in place: one, two, one, two . . .

[From the head of the line, a man screams: "twenty."]

— Oh, my belly hurts.
— Don't worry. Be patient.
Our turn will come soon.
The count has almost reached two hundred.

— Ooh! Aaaah! Aaah . . . Help!

[Amidst the crush and astonishment of women,
a newborn infant screams, and a woman weeps in pain.]

From *Clothes Like Paper*, 1992 [1983], 147–49.
*"Flying an elephant": an amazing, improbable achievement; a popular expression, often in ironic commentary, on a gathering crowd; "A hair from a bear": difficult to extract; also a popular expression [trans.].

— Here it is: your share. Take it and leave.
It is getting ugly here.

— Yes . . . but . . . can't you see: I have become two persons now, and these rations are still for one.

From the Street (1)

— Any news?
— It's the turn for milk today.
— Good! Better yet, it is for cigarettes, cheese, and tea.
— Tell me something about eggs.
— Ninety *tomans* for thirty.
If you don't get them at the black market,
you must live on turnips and garlic.

— Any news from the front?
— The usual: outrageous massacres by the enemy,
captives' cries.

— Any news of Yusof?*
— His letter came yesterday. The wolf has not devoured him.
But Abbas has gone to pieces.

— And Qodrat?†
— He is stuck at home, paralyzed in the legs.
The government isn't doing anything.
And his family is poor.

This is the fourth year of The War.
The News-at-Six said: peace was rejected.
This accords with the will of the old leader.

— Not many young ones are left.
— The war's reserves are the children.
Gradually this river will flow with blood.
— How long will this bloodshed last?
— As long as mothers give birth to children.

From *Clothes Like Paper,* 1992 [1983], 139–41.
*Cf. the story of Joseph, the well, the wolf, and the bloody shirt (Qoran, Sura 12) [trans.].
†A name meaning "power" [trans.].

— Tonight I will take the pill:
since giving birth is such a major sin.
— Me too . . . despite the desire. Enough is enough.

[Two peals of laughter burst like bullets on raw nerves.]

It Was the Pulse Flying

It was the pulse soaring, flying to the summit,
then plunging steeply below.
It was color abandoning lips,
leaving neither desire or a kiss.
The crimson blossom wilted.
The dark blue lily took its place.
Vision flew from the eyes,
leaving neither love or anger.
From the deep empty rings
farewells issued without greetings.
And the bird fluttered its wings and flew
to a place where the sun and the moon
awaited it with open arms.
The gates of heaven opened.
Flock of Angels proclaimed his arrival.
Heavenly residents sang salutations and greetings.
I thought, he arrived there, but too early,
in too much of a hurry.

I look at myself: I have stayed too late.
I wonder, what have I gained
from this lingering except exhaustion?
May the flesh fade from the memory,
its ashes scattered in the wind.
The flames have reached the warp and weft of this ancient satin.

From *A Window to Freedom*, 1995 [1983], 19–20. The poem is about the poet's grandson, Arzhan, dying from leukemia [author and trans.].

The World Is Shaped Like a Sphere

You have heard it.
You know about it.
The world is shaped like a sphere.
It has no left or right, the way you see it.
You can't take your bearings from a globe,
if with the flick of a finger you can make it turn
this way and that.
It was our agreement to call this the East,
though we could push it westward, with ease.
Don't speak to me of the West, where the sun sets,
if you always run after the sun,
you will never see a sunset.

The world divided by a line is a dead body cut in two
on which the vulture and the hyena are feasting.
You sit on the corpse with a crowd of flies
in self-contentment imagining
you are the host and patron.
A hyena snarl, the vulture flapping its wings
set the flies dancing in the air.
All that remains for you to do,
is to raise your hands to your head like a fly
and pray the prayer of stomachs.

From *A Window to Freedom*, 1995 [1981], 129–30.

Mind: Smoke Rings

Thoughts: smoke rings.
Thoughts: clouds. Pile upon pile.
At times winding: curl within curl.
At times unwinding: coil from coil.
Mind: tangle of braids, scarlet, yellow, green, and blue.
Ideas: fingers quivering, tying knots upon knots.
Eyes: tired of perpetual war between darkness and light.
Ears: worn down by perpetual noise and silence.
Heart: porcupine, taken refuge in my breast,
wearing out my body with its spines and restlessness.
Copper wires: molten, running through my body like nerves.
He who advises, bear it, has never experienced their heat.
He who filled my heart with hope
like a spectrum of light from beyond the clouds,
has turned into a spear piercing my eyes.
That liar, that corruption, that ogre from my childhood's tales
has escaped the vessel that contained him
and now appears at the window.
The canvas desire painted with all its art is in shreds:
the image did not last the rotting of the linen.
My tongue strays like a broken pen.
My trace dissolves like ink in water.

From *Plains of Arzhan*, 1983, 153–54.

Flog!

Flog! . . . One.
    Flog! . . . Two.
        Flog! . . . Three.
          Flog! . . . Four.
Watch it! Don't go over the prescribed count.*
Of that flower-clock at the square in Shiraz—
what do you remember?
Has it stopped ticking?
    Flog! . . . One.
        Flog! . . . Two.
          Flog! . . . Three.
            Flog! . . . Four.
It's different, this time. Amazing. Once again?
Tongue-tied. Small. Sheets of colored paper . . .
Father told me, count, count!
Father. Flower stalk. On a rock. In that year.
Brother. Bound. Patient. Captive.
Flog! . . . One.
    Flog! . . . Two.
        She screamed, my heart!
Oh, it's you, mother! With a sick heart?
Pale cheeks. Body cold.
Wooden coffin. Our last encounter.
Flog! . . . One.
    Flog! . . . Two.
        Oh, my head, my aching head.
Pain. Vertigo.
Such dark times and night on earth.
Woe.

From *Plains of Arzhan*, 1983, 149–51.

*As in a public flogging, administration of *hadd*, prescribed punishment for a variety of sins or infractions of dietary, sexual, moral and political order. *Bezan* is the command in Persian to strike, hit, flog. Here it is combined with the number of lashes [trans.].

From deep oblivion, an agitation, a gaze . . .
Myself. My desk. My office.
Myself. Ceiling. Wall.

It's Time to Mow the Flowers

It's time to mow the flowers,
don't procrastinate.
Fetch the sickles, come,
don't spare a single tulip in the fields.
The meadows in bloom:
who has ever seen such insolence?
The grass growing again:
step nowhere else but on its head.
Blossoms opening on every branch,
exposing the happiness in their hearts:
such colorful exhibitions must be stopped.
Bring your scalpels to the meadow
to cut out the eyes of flowers.
So that none may see or desire,
let not a seeing eye remain.
I fear the narcissus spreading its corruption:
stop its displays in a golden bowl
on a six-sided tray.
What is the use of your axe,
if not to chop down the elm tree?
In the maple's branches
allow not a single bird a moment's rest.
My poems and the wild mint
bear messages and perfumes.
Don't let them create a riot with their wild singing.
My heart is greener than green,
flowers sprout from the mud and water of my being.
Don't let me stand, if you are the enemies of Spring.

From *Plains of Arzhan*, 1983, 145–46.

Ears, Ears of Gold

There were ears, ears of gold,
fields, fields without end,
waves, waves of shadow and light,
undulations of a silken breeze.
And thump-thumped the blossoms' heart
in the happy sunlight.
And golden sequins glittered
on the branches of pines.
And in deep blue waters
wondrous colors swiftly flowed.
And on swimmer's skins glistened
scales of star-washed silver.

Then a little black fish grew *and grew* . . .
to become a symbol in the discourse of the elite,
an emblem for their mighty deeds.
It was rumored, it had received its strength
from the twin magicians of Babylon.
Under the eyes of the incredulous
it became a leviathan of mountainous size:
opening its mouth like the jaws of hell
to swallow the sun and the Eastern sky
in darkness.

From *Plains of Arzhan*, 1983 [1982], 141–42.

There were no more fields
or golden ears,
only curtains remained,
and the houses of sleep,
and the salt from my tears,
and the din of the coppersmiths' hammer.*

---

*An allusion perhaps to the myth of origin of *aruz* (meters) in Arabic and Persian poetry, according to which Khalil Ibn Ahmad, inspired by the rhythms of the coppersmiths' hammer in the bazaar of Basra, "invented" a core of fifteen meters, to which many were added later. See Mohamad Fesharaki, "Az Khalil Ta Simin (From Khalil to Simin)," in *Simin Behbahani,* special edition of *Nimeye Digar* 2, no. 1 (1993): 67–82 [trans.].

A Bat or Some Other Creature

In a cave's deep obscurity
lurks a bat or some other creature
with menacing teeth and claws.
Something slithers up my sides and back,
cold and wet against my warm skin.
Oh, oh, it's a snake, I think!
In the dark, two red sparks
glare like the eyes of a beast or a monster,
perhaps on the scent of its prey.
I hear the water dripping drop by drop
monotonously, without stop,
from the cave's hangings
to the jagged floor below.
The stench of rot and slime and decaying flesh
fill the heart of the cave.
Never has a fresh breeze found its way here.
My arms are not strong enough to repel harm,
nor my feet free enough to flee.
In the immensity of my horror
I compose and chant a myth or a slogan,
a fable or a fighting poem,
thinking I shall endure hoping
for that final deliverance:
tomorrow, when the knight will rise
from the seed in the water.*

But they sing the same refrain,
the bats and the beasts,
the snakes and the monsters,
"You wait in vain, you wait in vain."

From *Plains of Arzhan*, 1982 [1983], 139–40.

*In Zoroastrian eschatology seed/sperm in the water evokes the figure of the avenging messiah(s), of which there are three, one for each millennium after Zoroaster, the final one being the Soshiant. Each is born from Zoroaster's sperm, preserved in the waters of a lake, to impregnate at the right time three virgin mothers destined to bear them [trans.].

You Said, It's Only Grapes

You said, it's only grapes. I said, I don't see any!
You said, believe me. I will pick you some.
This is the garden of history and these the vines
that bear fruit each year in great abundance and variety.
You gestured with your hands as if you were picking grapes.
I said, this isn't something to joke about.
You said, close your eyes and open your mouth.
I will let you taste one that is firm and sweet.
I did as you told me. Ugh! How salty it was!
It tasted of vomit and blood. I spat it out.
It was an extracted eyeball.
It was as if the ceiling had collapsed on my head.
It was as if the world had started rolling like a millstone.
It was as if the stars and the moon were raining blood.
You said, it's only grapes. I screamed,
on the vines, I see nothing else but eyeballs.

From *Plains of Arzhan*, 1983 [1982], 137–38.

I Used to Tell You

I fear snakes, I used to tell you.
They really frighten me,
I would repeat, again and again.
When you played with a rope
pretending it was a snake,
I would tell you, agitated,
what you do frightens me.
When you tied the false snakes
to your shoulders, I would scream,
take them off, they frighten me!
When you declared, Zahak, that's me,*
I groaned in pain: heartless,
cowardly, murderous, cannibal,
I am frightened.
You laughed and said, it's just a game.
I said, games that end in massacres
frighten me.

The snakes came to life.
Your laughter turned to terror.
You clung to my skirt begging,
stop this, I am frightened!
I shook my head in helplessness
and spoke with anguished eyes:
now I *have* to be frightened.
To survive you have ripped out
so many brains.
Now snakes do not frighten me
as much as the loved one.

From *Plains of Arzhan*, 1983 [1982], 129–30.

*Archetypal tyrant from the *Shahnameh*, king-turned-monster by a demon's kiss on the shoulders, from which two snakes grew, demanding to be fed every day the brains of two Iranian youths, in exchange for not torturing the king [trans.].

Must Write Something

Must write something, must, but where?
To find a notebook or tablet, where?
Must write a poem, but pray tell,
to find ears for a good poem, where?
Must tell tales of another Rostam.
But with Rostam found, to find Raksh,* where?
Must run nonstop if legs permit.
But given the strength, from here to where?

Must write something, but with what pen?
They have smashed everything.
To find even a splinter, where?
One must offer like them one's blood, life, and honor.
But to find the strength for it, where?
I understand, one must give up on finding sugarcane.
But even to find hemlock or colocynth in this desert, where?

Tell Plato to make another design:
"never" is his architect in "nowhere."

From *Plains of Arzhan*, 1983 [1982], 103–4.

*Raksh is Rostam's wonder-horse, his closest and necessary companion and the only horse capable of bearing his weight. Horse and rider shine forth in the epic *Shahnameh* [trans.].

My Country, I Will Build You Again

To the lady of Persian story telling, Simin Daneshvar

My country, I will build you again,
if need be, with bricks made from my life.
I will build columns to support your roof,
if need be, with my bones.
I will inhale again the perfume of flowers
favored by your youth.
I will wash again the blood off your body
with torrents of my tears.
Once more, the darkness will leave this house.
I will paint my poems blue with the color of our sky.
The resurrector of "old bones"* will grant me in his bounty
a mountain's splendor in his testing grounds.
Old I may be, but given the chance, I will learn.
I will begin a second youth alongside my progeny.
I will recite the Hadith of "love of country"†
with such fervor as to make each word bear life.
There still burns a fire in my breast
to keep undiminished the warmth of kinship
I feel for my people.
Once more you will grant me strength,
though my poems have settled in blood.
Once more I will build you with my life,
though it be beyond my means.

From *Plains of Arzhan*, 1983 [1982], 97–98.

*Or "Azm-e Ramim," Qoranic reference to the day of resurrection, when God will reconstitute human beings from their rotten bones (Sura 36:78, "Ya Seen") [trans.].

†Refers to a Hadith (a "Tradition" or account of the Prophet, his companions or the Imams) known as *hubb al-watan* or "Love of country/homeland," in which the Prophet is reported to have said, "*hubb al-watan min al iman*" or "Love of country/homeland is from faith." [trans.].

Sounds of Blossoms

My heart is more broken than the crystal cup you let drop on the rocks.

—Khaghani

Hear the Spring in my body,
Hear the blossoms opening like the Pleiades,
singing, it's me, it's me.
Hear my drunken declaration: a wild rose, that's me.
Why should I wait any longer to play the lyre of Aphrodite?
Hear me plucking its veins in a thousand modes.
Each of my veins is now the string of an instrument:
hear their music rising and descending.
Hear me playing myself, singing, *tantananam, tantananam.**
This soaring, overflowing joy—is it me? No, not me!
Hear once more the old wine sparkling in the wine jar.
Gaze in my eyes at consciousness flourishing like a garden.
Hear a world of awakenings dormant in my words.
Hear the world awakening in my words.
You fill my body and soul like a pearl filling its shell.
Hear your own words, said and unsaid, on my lips.
For I am both the drunken gypsy
and the precious cup in your hand.
Hear your rivals gasp at the waste as I fall.
Hear the shattering sounds, my stonehearted one,
hear the sounds of my falling and liberation,
hear my cut glass body.

From *Plains of Arzhan*, 1983 [1981], 85–86.

*Ostensibly meaningless (perhaps with semantic reverberations), words put to rhythmic, incantatory, musical use, in one of Rumi's ecstatic poems [trans.].

My Heart Is Heavy, Friend

My heart is heavy, friend. I feel like crying.
If I escape this cage, where will I go?
Where will I go, since I know no path to any garden?
Since I opened my eyes, it has been to a dead end.
I have given my heart to no one.
No one has given his heart to me.
I have drifted like a piece of driftwood
freely upon the waves.
Persons who were distant I held close,
as my heart is to my breast.
Persons close I held at a distance, faraway.
Neither does my heart expect to receive anyone,
neither do I have the wine to drink to a friend's memory.
What did my being add to the sum of existence?
What would my nonbeing subtract from it?
Who will tell me I am alive and for what purpose?
I have hidden the stars in a cloudy sky.
My heart is heavy, my friend. I feel like crying.

From *Plains of Arzhan*, 1983 [1982], 69–70.

Song (5)

Gypsy, you need not accept everything he says.
Listen to someone else for a change.
Go, if he said, "don't go"—may your feet be swift.
Don't come, if he said, "come"—may your ears be hard of hearing.

From *Plains of Arzhan*, 1983, 57.

Song (4)

With thoughts of murder, your heart has dwelt in your body for a lifetime.
What has your heart been but a snake hiding in a shirt?
It has embellished its crown with Mars and its wings with rainbows.
Your heart is beautiful. But it is a fighting cock.

From *Plains of Arzhan*, 1983, 56.

Song (3)

Gypsy, blindness has been your reward for crying.
Separation has crushed your heart.
You have always seen him through tamed eyes.
Look at him once as a drunken camel.

From *Plains of Arzhan*, 1983, 55.

Gypsiesque (15)

Gypsy, weep again. Madness is on the rise.
The cry repressed will kill you. Scream! Howl!
Love is your very being. It holds your soul hostage.
Why deny yourself? Climb the rooftop, proclaim it!
Your body and soul have caught fire,
haven't you muffled your voice long enough?
Your radiant soul has darkened,
draw this curtain back.
The "*haq haq*"* bird demands the truth:
are you less than a nocturnal bird?
Break your wall of silence,
call out: lover! beloved!
Wrestling with your rebellious flesh,
rip things, break things, pull them by the roots.
Tear your heart out of your chest
and smash it on the brow of waiting.
No, your meddling heart deserves greater torture:
grab it by the ears, take it to the street, and hang it!
No, no, may you never commit such madness:
because this phosphorescent mixture of fire and blood is a gift.
Make a gem from it to decorate the crown of the times.
No, no, it's a flower, this heart of yours:
it looks good on your sash.
Put it to good use, stick it with a pin, and wear it.
No, no, keep it, till the time of the rendezvous,
then throw it like a hunted bird at the spear
of the man on horseback.

From *Plains of Arzhan*, 1983, 47–48.

*Cries of a nocturnal bird, meaning "truth, truth." The bird itself is called *morq-e haq*, truth-bird [trans.].

Gypsiesque (13)

Sing, gypsy, sing.
In homage to being you must sing.
Let ears register your presence.
Eyes and throats burn from the smoke
that trails the monsters as they soar in the sky.
Scream if you can of the terrors of this night.
Every monster has the secret of his life
hidden in a bottle in the stomach of a red fish
swimming in waters you cannot reach.
In her lap every maid holds a monster's head
like a piece of firewood set in silver.
In their frenzy to plunder, the monsters
have plundered the beautiful maidens
of the silk and rubies of their lips and cheeks.

Gypsy, stamp your feet.
For your freedom stamp your feet.
To get an answer,
send a message with their beat.
To your existence there must be a purpose under heaven.
To draw a spark from these stones,
stamp your feet.
Ages dark and ancient
have pressed their weight against your body.
Break out of their embrace,
lest you stay a mere trace in a fossil.

Gypsy, to stay alive, you must slay silence.
I mean, to pay homage to being, you must sing.

From *Plains of Arzhan*, 1983 [1982], 43–44.

Gypsiesque (14)

To Hashem Javid

Gypsy, hide your heart in the closet,
lest its echoing love songs break the silence.
A bird of amazement is this heart:
crush its ruby beak, lest it pick stars
like seeds from the sky.
The chief's crown needs more red feathers:
the wings of this vagabond bird
are soaked in blood.
With love, with love, with love,
do not give yourself away.
Burn like a letter thrown unread in the fire.
Sign your sad letters with a finger
dipped in your sad heart,
leaving no other trace of yourself
to be gazed upon by a stranger.
Such unhidden crying will stain your reputation:
make counterfeit, unprovoked laughter,
to put even a mask to shame.
Centuries of oppression have seeped into your bones,
beyond the powers of time to drain.
Gypsy, a leprous Spring has set camp
on the plains of your soul:
what else fills your ulcerous blossoms
but the pus of hatred?
In your eyes every flower is a wound
with five bloody petals,
every swaying branch is a seven-tailed whip.
Gypsy, you asked a friend, what signifies truth.
Her profound answer was: perpetual silence.

From *Plains of Arzhan*, 1983 [1982], 45–46.

Gypsiesque (1)

The gypsy tells a fortune, full of promises:
in thirty days . . . thirty weeks . . . thirty months . . .
But where is my patience for even thirty seconds?
Have you no herb, gypsy, for my love-pains?
From things that grow gypsies make remedies.
Gypsy, have you no prayer for me or a talisman?
My nanny used to tell me gypsies can write prayers
that can solve any problem.
Gypsy, find out if love's flame still burns
in his tongue and breast, even if small.
Even if the woman sharing his bed
has the face of Scheherazade,
is she as wondrous a storyteller,
whispering stories of love in his ears?
O gypsy, my heart is torn.
Take me with you from this land,
if there be a place in your tribe for a stranger.
Gypsy, I have poems as delicate
as snakes' eyelashes.
What is their worth there, such merchandise?
Gypsy, you haven't answered me,
only echoed everything I've said.
Is it fair to mock and make fun
of anyone as weary as me?

I am the gypsy, oh, yes.
Here there is no one else but me.
The gypsy's image is visible
as long as I face the mirror.

From *Plains of Arzhan*, 1983 [1982], 19–20.

Tick Tock, Tick Tock

Tick tock, Tick tock.
Oh, how the instant moves,
humbly, by compulsion, on its path.
Stay still, my life, stay!
Oh, God, I need a respite.
It goes without a word, a farewell, or a parting look.
It goes like water from a spring, instants dropping,
drop after drop, turning to a month, then a year,
and in a year and a month moving on.
It rises with the sun, in shimmering gold.
It sinks with the bleeding sunset in a well.
As soon as I have covered my mind
with the silk of sleep, a spell of light arrives
and a spell of darkness leaves,
stamping my life with stripes of black and white
with their coming and going.
The traveler on this road is me.
For me there is no turning back.
Woe is me. Tell my life, its going is ill-timed.
The hammer of my pulse is tired of counting.
Oh . . . oh . . . my life goes . . . instant by instant.

From *A Trajectory of Speed and Fire*, 1981 [1980], 137–38.

Love Came So Red

Love came so red, though it came late.
How breathtaking: a red flower growing in the snow.
O love, how far am I from the mountaintop?
How ancient are my hands! How shaky my feet!
O friend, I fear love shivering from a breeze,
doubts dissolving its image on the water.
The young cactus is born in the tropics:
I am an arctic desert, with a frigid climate in my breast.
My heart is swollen, too large for its cocoon.
It wants to fly, but its wings have rotted in confinement.
It is late now, too late.
She who walked, her arms laden with faith,
now suffers by necessity the poverty of faithlessness.
She who hopped and skipped like a doe,
is calm and quiet now, a tame sheep.
She who wore her pride like a rainbow,
now shyly hides her head in a shell.
Love, crimson flame, my ashen despair
reflects your last glow.

From *A Trajectory of Speed and Fire*, 1981 [1980], 135–36.

You Leave, I'll Stay

To those who left.
To those who stayed behind.

You leave, I'll stay. You leave, I'll stay.
I swear, I cannot endure being separated from my homeland.
Till my last day you will hear in my bonesill
the same "tale of the reed."*
Though sparkles and light may fill the nights of exile,
they are of little use to me, since I am not happy in exile.
From the agitation of fire and molten metal
the sky above me is as turbulent as my mind.
When one must cover the light in a lamp,
I would rather extinguish the flame
than let my ears be pierced by the policeman's orders,
"lights out!" "black out!"†
Where will my heart escape,
if this house and its shade collapse on my head?
In these dark ruins we remain:
the children, the old people, and I,
and our sad cares and thoughts of absent, brave warriors.
I will not forsake this unruly corner to beg for affection
in a land of self-serving calculation.
Even if this sky is dark and unsmiling,
it belongs to me and my fellow countrymen.
This canopy is not on loan.
Hoping for a better day,
I take one step, then another,
towards something I believe.
You leave, I'll stay.

From *A Trajectory of Speed and Fire*, 1981 [1980], 133–34.

*Opening lines of Rumi's *Mathnavi*, well known as any lines of poetry by Iranians: "Hear the tales told by the reed / complaining of separations // From the time I was cut from the reedbed / men and women have cried with me in sympathy" [trans.].

†The time frame of this poem is the war with Iraq, when blackouts and their enforcement were issues of everyday life for many Iranians [trans.].

Dry, Lifeless, Dry

Dry, lifeless, dry.
Devotion dry. Womb dry.
Such dryness and sterility
cannot give birth to even something dry:
not a proud, dancing stalk,
not even a thorn anywhere in this dry desert.
I dread abandoning love:
its flower fresh and damp.
Sadly, I must leave, with my hands dry, skirt dry.
The master screams musts and must nots,
his face and tone bitter, his prescriptions dry,
his prohibitions dry,
his curses and complaints dry,
his sermons and contritions dry,
always saying the same thing,
killing me with their monotony.
I try to divine my fortune
from the sediments of my morning coffee:
I can only see dried-up blood clots
on the sides of the cup.
O heart, turn your eyes of expectation
away from these people,
since their benevolence has long been dry,
as dry as their faith and reason.
The harp has lost its voice, the flute its song,
but rejoice: for they provide dry firewood for the winter.
The ringdoves with their green songs
have lost their spirit and cannot fly,
in this blazing Tamuz*
their throats are parched dry.
I am thirsty, O Muslims.
If you truly follow your faith, I seek water,
water in this desert, burning, dry.

From *A Trajectory of Speed and Fire*, 1981 [1980], 119–20.
*June–July in the Syriac calendar [trans.].

O Child of Today

O child of today, if you love war,
I am the child of yesterday,
I loathe war.
Since I found this world steeped in blood and madness
I have made my principle to dispute war.
It is hard for feet worn out by the endless desert
to tolerate these stones and thorns.
Don't talk to me of this fratricidal tribe
that takes delight in the sight of blood,
because today my heart is heavy.
How long can one keep on asking,
is this a hand, is this is a finger?
How long can one look and wonder,
is this an arm, is this an elbow?
These are good days for the vultures and hyenas,
with the bodies of the killed so many
and so close at hand.
The wounded moaning make our choral song,
the death spasms of the dying our collective dance.
What has become of that reviving tenderness
in the heart of nature?
Its only remaining sign is a carpet of moss on the rocks.
Purify it with water. Perfume it with the rose's essence.
You cannot wash out blood stains with blood.
For ignoring the commandment,
"cast not yourself by your hands into destruction"*
you are cursed to shed your bodies
in battlefield carnage.

From *A Trajectory of Speed and Fire*, 1981 [1980], 113–14.

*Qoran, Sura 2:191, quotation translated by A. J. Arberry, *The Koran Interpreted* (New York: Macmillan, 1955), 54 [trans.].

Time, It Is Dream Time

Time—it is dream time,
time without order or coherence,
time of agitated signs,
of ambiguous appearances.
It's the time without time,
when you can see stillness
invade the fleeting moment.
It's the time of all times,
when you can return once more
to the old tales of history,
to ancient darkness.
It's the time when years of endured pain
fit in the volume of an instant,
when a cold sigh rushes
down the length of the century.
Time, it is dream time,
when you cannot choose or distinguish
between life and death,
when thought and image have lost all measure,
unbound by any discipline or style,
when you sit in a cloud sprinkling stars,
when you reach for the moon
to squeeze an orange,
when to escape a crocodile's teeth
you wish to throw yourself
upside down in a well,
but you lack the strength.
With hands tied behind your back,
what knots can you unravel?
With feet weary of stones,
what road can you travel?
Time, it is dream time,

From *A Trajectory of Speed and Fire*, 1981 [1979], 111–12.

when diviners of horror
are cheerfully busy mourning.
Wherefore, O lord, such pestilence
after pestilence in our dreams?
Wherefore these shadows?*

........................†

---

*Shadow, as in "Shadow of God," familiar epithet for Iranian kings [trans.].

†Dotted line in the original, censored or deleted. For a discussion of meanings, conventions, and rhetoric of dotted lines in Persian literature, the reader might refer to *Suppressed Persian: An Anthology of Forbidden Literature,* by Paul Sprachman (Costa Mesa, Calif.: Mazda, 1995), xxxii–xxxiii [trans.].

Barren Desert

"And his eyes turned white from grief"*

When the night falls on the barren desert,
two women in black pray for the rain
and strew stars by the fistful,
hoping they will sprout.
Two women with lit torches seek the light
yet are lost for ever in the dark.
Two women complain to the mirror about fortune,
blaming it for all their sorrows.
Like two springs, two women
water the desert with their tears,
turning it into a salt marsh, a garden of thorns.
Two women, like two angels, hope to return,
their long wait proving their faith.
On the path, it seems, two women in black
are changing into white.†

From *A Trajectory of Speed and Fire*, 1981 [1979], 109–10.
*Qoran, Sura 12:83, "Joseph."
†As in the Persian expression, eyes turning white or blind from crying [trans.].

Doubts, Doubts, Doubts

Doubts, doubts, doubts, at dusk,
when you can't tell wolf and sheep apart,
when a sickly, jaundiced, light
has spread itself on the dirt of the threshold.
The gray line on the horizon:
what is it blowing our way?
Is this the lead of the lies of the night
or the silver of the dawn's truth?
Uncertain, full of dread, the traveler ponders
at the threshold of his journey,
"shall I wait or begin?"
O Blood! O Blood! A hundred times, blood!
That ball of lead, messenger of death,
has found its way into every heart,
made eyes burst, brains scatter,
and the blood boil on the rocks
and thistles on the road.
It does not come easy to re-enact that battle
"in every land, every day." *
Who are these people to that challenger of dread?
What is this place to that place of dread?
Once there was a place where truth was pure and absolute.
Right and wrong have been mixed since,
everywhere, always.
With doubts settled in the shelter of the eyes,
faith will repudiate truth
even if it shows its face.

From *A Trajectory of Speed and Fire*, 1981 [1979], 107–8.

*A popular refrain during the early days of the Revolution, implying every day could be Ashura, when Imam Hossein and his family were martyred; every place could be Karbela, the battlefield where they were martyred [author and trans.].

Can You Really Fly?

Can you really fly, O bird,
you who have known bondage?
Will you prefer to fight, O lion,
you who have known chains?
What difference would it make
if you could not fly?
Feathers and wings of conviction will suffice
for you who have learned to fly high.
Not for you the lyre's complains,
you with a stone's resilience.
There will be no crying
by the rock accustomed to the pickax.
You were once a maple tree,
thick with branches of your beliefs.
You stood tall by the crossroad,
learning from a thousand calamities.
No dawn pillows or silk sheets for you
who have long taught your body other tastes.
Comforts will shame you
who have learned the ways of hardship.
A life of ease you relinquish to bystanders,
you whose feet have bled on the path of honor.
Your enemies have gained more chains,
your friends more wisdom from their pains.
In the fires I shunned, you made your home,
you who have learned from the wild rue
the ecstasy of self-immolation.
Speaking of the hard life in prison
will not come easily to me.
One cannot speak of such bitter things
with lips accustomed to sugar.

From *A Trajectory of Speed and Fire*, 1981 [1978], 91–92. Poem written on the occasion of the freeing of the first group of prisoners in Aban, 1357 (November 1978) [author and trans.].

This poem is unworthy of you,
though for a lifetime Simin has taught
your ways and principles
in her ghazals.

I Can't Look

I can't look: a corpse lies on the ground,
its horrifying outline punctuated by bullets,
the swamp bubbles that were his eyes
expelled from their sockets,
emptied of all joy and sadness,
separated from all hatred and love.
From breast to Adam's apple
not a breath stirs in or out.
It's a cold path, emptied of its last lament.
He whose ring had a gem stained with blood,
has empty sockets for eyes,
like rings with their stones extracted.
I cannot bear looking at him fallen so low,
despite the wise man's council
that such is the enemy's just deserts.
But God knows, even if beaten senseless by the enemy,
I would not consent to his murder:
for this is my religion.
O Lord, my good Lord, why did you create evil?
Why would one who prefers virtue
create evil?
Would it have mattered if human beings were made
with the temperament of angels?
How can something pure emerge
from impure clay?*
My curses upon Cain's soul:
he may have started it.
But on Gabriel's soul I swear:
this will not end it.
"The Book, The Scale, and The Iron"
are verses heaven sent to guide us.†

From *A Trajectory of Speed and Fire*, 1981 [1978], 101–2.
*Qoran, creation of human beings from clay (Sura 55:14) [trans.].
†Qoran, verses on laws, judgments, and punishments (Sura 42:17) [trans.].

But this is "Justice" with a dagger in its sleeves.
From justice, too, I flee,
since it too represents oppression.
"Justice" is needed where oppression rules.

What a Cold and Somber Silence

For Arzhan Gharun

What a cold and somber silence!
What a cold and somber silence!
With no respite for a downpour of tears.
With no light from a sigh's flame.
With not a scratch on your face to disclose your weariness inside.
With no cry from your breast to reveal a broken heart.
What else but crimson blossoms from a wounded flower?
What else but a piece of lead rushes from an ambush at a turn in a road?
Why not let the breeze in the street of martyrs carry your greetings?
It has blown over a plain without plants or flowers,
so often closing its eyes in horror, biting its lips in amazement.
It has traveled where words carry no auspicious tidings,
where no meanings reside in a glance.
If you see the glint of bayonets, warn me about bullets.
Beside their light there is no other,
no starlight or moonlight in the night of the henchman.
From behind the curtain gaze at the shrine of real men:
how many heads were lost fighting for a hat!
I am left with my cries and curses of loathing.
When I scream, O God . . . you answer, Amen.

From *A Trajectory of Speed and Fire*, 1981 [1978], 87–88.

So Long in This Old Land

"I am tired of this more than sixty years
of moving, night and day"

—Naser Khosrow

So long have I lingered in this old land,
had my fill of life to satiation,
that even though not sixty yet,
I believe I have lingered too long.
I am the blighted blossom in the flower garden
that aged before tasting youth.
I am the tired lily that stood on one leg,
patiently, in this pool, for a long time,
with no one aware of my inner displays.
I am the imaginary figure left in the unconscious.
I had no sooner raised my head from the egg's shell
when I found myself trapped in a narrow cage.
Two men have bound me, and shackled to each one
I have been a willing slave for a while.
The chains of one had hardly broken
when I was a slave chained by another master.
One gave me a name, the other love.
Thus have I remained an abject pawn.

From *A Trajectory of Speed and Fire*, 1981 [1977], 65–66.

I Sell Souls

> Don't play with fire,
> if your house is made of reeds.
>
> —Sa'di

I sell souls, that is my merchandise,
of all things contemptible, the most vile.
In the city of self-worshippers,
in the quarter where baseness rules,
this has long been the passion and profit.
To find shelter and protect life and limb,
this has been the first and last resort.
For the essence I killed with degradation
now my sleeves are moist with tears of mourning.
I saw blasphemous verses, heard insane rebukes,
then declared them without shame
to be ordered by reason and religion.
I am the gem atop the ring of the silent,
since silence is every gem's command.
A bloody tempest rages in my heart
from "walking away and turning a blind eye."*
It has made the Chinese gazelle†
transform into an owl.
I wish the garden of my eyes to flourish,
but these clusters of tears are its choicest vines.
What do you call this night: endless horror?
What falls on my roof: snow of fright?
My spirit is frigid. There is ice in my bones,
as if my home were the deepest arctic.

From *A Trajectory of Speed and Fire*, 1981 [1976], 49–50.

*Referring to the order once issued to the public (with contemporary generalized and metaphorical applications) on the approach of kings and their entourage, especially "their" women: literally, "Walk away! Go blind!" [trans.].

†Things Chinese are often associated in Persian literature with beauty, fineness [trans.].

I console myself: at least you have matches,
fiery poems to raise a hundred flames.
But Sa'di councils, extinguish these flames:
don't play with fire
if your house is made of reeds.

Metamorphosis

Our metamorphosis was such
that it made our forest-dwelling,
scarlet-buttocked ancestor
weep for us.
On us were bestowed horns and tails
so that no other beast could take our place.
Defying the skeptics' incredulity,
we flaunted four black hooves
on our hands and legs.
Our hairy robes of honor
drew compliments from our friends.
We were driven to the meadows
roped and prodded like beasts.
Our lust to graze choked the "why?" in our throats.
Our swamp-like eyes accepted no other reflection
but of the grass at our feet.
They are like screams rising from our throats:
how do our prayers differ now
from our curses?
They did to us what is done to the beasts of the field:
branded us where I am ashamed to tell.
Now we grow old, male and female,
with the milk and the plow,
till the butcher decides which knife
we best deserve.

From *A Trajectory of Speed and Fire*, 1981 [1975], 31–32.

O Box Within Box

O box within box, walls that enclose me,
one day I will escape this onion-like confinement.
One day I will wash my frail body in the light
and let the sun clothe me with its golden robe.
One day the flash of dawn on my green spear
will stir me to battle.
I will rise, in slow increments.
I will make my face beautiful
like a mirror held to the rainbow.
I will scatter blue petals in the wind,
let my silk scarf flutter in abandon,
and like an Iris praise God in the mountains.
·O onion-like walls, one day, when the morning
holds up to me its mirror without rust,
I will find myself suddenly in full bloom
and you doomed to rot.

From *A Trajectory of Speed and Fire*, 1981 [1974], 25–26.

Laws of Lead

With such laws of lead,
I am silent by necessity.
I applaud every ugliness.
I accept every degradation.
If I could send a silent, wordless message,
I would ask for bitter hemlock:
it would be sweet to me.
A gray death is the choice of the ruby flame.
Like that I will burn a while,
then quietly expire.
In this perpetual Fall
I am a vine without a trellis:
too far from any thing to lean on,
too late for resurrection.

O tall trees, "clutching at the eyes of the stars," *
I am a tiny branch in fear
of the old woodcutters,
trembling for my reputation,
tired of always yielding
like a shadow in a pool.
You would think they have tied
a rock around my neck,
the way I scrape and bow
like a humble slave
displaying respect to her masters.

From *A Trajectory of Speed and Fire,* 1981 [1974], 19–20.

*Refers to lines in "The Other Song," a poem by Manuchehr Atashi: "I am not like Hafez, immortalized in songs . . . / I am Ibn-e Yamin, clutching at the eyes of the stars / I am Masʾud-e Saʾd, wishing for a window" [author]. The latter figures personify extreme confinement: Ibn-e Yamin, Biblical Benjamin, falsely accused, imprisoned, and held hostage in Egypt by Joseph to teach his other brothers a lesson and send his father, Jacob, a message; and Masʾud-e Saʾd, poet and panegyrist, who spent fifteen years imprisoned in India (died H. 515/1137) [trans.].

Life, O burdensome patience,
I count the minutes with the beatings of a heart
that has filled me with you to satiation.
There is no awakening for me
from this hypnotic sleep.
Whoever the demon, I will worship him.
Whatever he commands, I will obey.

I Want a Cup of Sin

He said I want that which cannot be found.

—Mowlavi

I want a cup of sin, a cup of corruption,
and some clay mixed with darkness,
from which I shall mold an image shaped like man,
wooden-armed and straw-haired.

His mouth is big.
He has lost all his teeth.
His looks reflect his ugliness within.
Lust has made him violate all prohibitions
and to grow on his brow an "organ of shame."*
His eyes are like two scarlet beams,
one focused on a sack of gold,
the other on the pleasures found in bed.
He changes masks like a chameleon,
has a two-timing heart like an eel.
He grows tall like a giant branch,
as if his body has acquired vegetable properties.

Then, he will come to me,
intent on my oppression.
I will protest and scream against his horror.
And that ogre called man
will tame me with his insults.

As I gaze into his eyes
innocently and full of shame,
I will scold myself: you see,
how you spent a lifetime wishing for "Adam."†
Here you have what you asked for.

From *A Trajectory of Speed and Fire*, 1981 [1973], 13–14.

Sharm-gah, or "the place of shame," a euphemism for genitals [trans.].

†*Adam* in Persian is generic for human being as well as the name of Eve's husband [trans.].

Don't Read

To Mohammad Behbahani

Don't read these deceptions made by the hands of Satan
even if they seem to be verses from Heaven.
Not many of these false-Marys will remain,
once you have unmasked the shameless whores.
You cannot believe a field of sunflowers
to be a congregation of suns.
The illusory warmth of a few glowworms
have not warmed the breath of this winter's night.
They are only tinseled, these leaves and flowers
tied to these naked branches.
This is not the sky but a painting on a ceiling
on which glows a painted sun.
This is but a performance in which from behind a curtain
someone makes these lifeless shadows dance.
Where are my childhood's beliefs
in the stories of princes and monsters,
beliefs that were clear as a mirror or water?
I weep for the death of my beliefs
that had no intimation yet
of human beings.

From *A Trajectory of Speed and Fire*, 1981 [1973], 9–10.

The Dead Are Silent

Under that tall golden dome,
around that sanctuary without blemish,
dust lies on people's breasts,
stones lie on the dust.

The day hides behind the night's veil.
The night sleeps, sunk in silence.
Not even the dagger of an owl's cries
pierces the heart of the silence.

Not a dead man plays a skull-drum
with a shin bone.
You cannot hear a moan, or a murmur,
or a humming in the heart of the night.
I have heard about the dance of the dead.
But what corpse can shake a hand or leg?
Of all who sleep in this prison of silence,
not one has broken out of its coffin.

Worms have nestled in the eye sockets of one.
Snakes have made their nest in the skull of another.
Sediments have clogged the arteries of one.
The sinews of another have lost their power.

The caretaker arrives, quietly,
a proud and stupid grin on his face.
His rewards are the fruits of death,
his strolling grounds, graves' breasts.

From *Resurrection*, 1981 [1979], 103–5.

He exhorts the dead
(and no one complains).
Rest in peace! Here is my bread
waiting for your *halvah*.*

---

*A kind of sweetmeat or paste distributed customarily at shrines and graveyards to commemorate the dead [trans.].

Workshop

These eyes made of glass, who made them?
These eyes without expectation,
on whose path are they fixed?
This army of figurines, with the silence of death,
left behind in the workshop,
whose souvenirs are they?
Look at these windup toys merrily dancing,
around whose axis do they spin?
These paper boats made by childish hands,
what breeze do they await, from what land?
These cardboard horsemen mouthing epics,
whom do they seek to battle?
The medals they wear, these lifeless wooden figures,
of what glories do they boast?
The hearts of the children of this city
waiting to be molded like sculpture's clay,
whose hands do they await to mold them?
The moss covering these humble ruins,
whose springtime rapture has made them grow?
In the light of your lamps there are nothing but lies,
for whom does my true sun hold a mirror?

From *Resurrection*, 1973, 77–78.

Lead Insulation

Why do I vainly chain my eyes,
drunk or sober, to the wall clock?
Let the black-faced dancers you call hands
dance a while on the rusty surface.
Too weak to wander, they sit and wait,
like the leg of a captive caught in a trap.
It is as if time had frozen,
its flowing mirror still, like winter ice.
There are ears to hear but no sounds,
eyes to see but no beauty,
except for groans of frustration,
verses of despair.
This curtain of darkness, this dust of forgetfulness,
has come to conceal evil
like lead insulation.
In deep sleep people seek and wander,
running each way,
with their souls playthings of a disease.
Death comes to the weak creatures
still asleep in their silk cocoons,
granting them not a moment's wakefulness.
It is as if blood had stopped circulating
in the arteries of time.
It's as if the heart had stopped beating
in the wall clock.

From *Resurrection*, 1973, 73–74.

Lead Dust

Why should the earth be a field of arrows?
Why should the sky be drenched in blood?
Why should this be the custom everywhere,
from earth to sky?
Why should my eyelids always shut the door to joy?
Why should crystals grow from tears on my lashes?
If by effort I see no chance to become master,
why do I stoop to abject slavery?
If I could not behold the light
in the mirror of the firmaments,
why is my vision reduced to the dust
gathering on the steel walls?
If those sitting on thrones had no chance to gallop,
why did our heroes come to ride wooden horses?
It's as if lead dust is falling from the sky.
Why, O God, must the air that sustains us be so heavy?
Why must praise clothe deception?
Why must prayers take root in the blood of curses?
If my singing did not give power to a superman,
why did it become a death-song
over a bloodstained corpse?
Words dying in breasts, tongues rotting in mouths,
not a cry escapes our lips—
O God, why should it be like this?

From *Resurrection*, 1973, 71–72.

Apples, Crimson Lanterns

Don't beat me like this
with the bones of the dead
upon my head.
For God's sake, stop this beating,
give me an hour's rest.
O you who earn your bread
like morticians from the dead,
don't decorate your chest and shoulders
with their backbones.
Don't become the graveyard bat,
hiding in the dark,
flapping your wings by my bed
every night like death.
Count me not as one of your own,
putting me to shame as you have yourself.
Don't try to graft thorns
on the moist musk-willow.
Such were the injuries
that broke the apple's crimson lanterns.
Don't throw lies like rocks
at the fruit-laden branch.
Stop this hail of slanders
like bullets aimed at every heart.
When I have squeezed
the grapes of my eyes into bottles,
do not drink my tears laughing,
as if you were drinking a cup of wine.
My mind is positive, free of conjectures,
my voice an eternal echo.
Do not assault my convictions
with your doubts.

From *Resurrection*, 1973, 67–68.

Maybe It Is the Messiah

The horizon is pregnant,
its womb filled with the seed of light.
The issue of this blind darkness is the sun.
Tomorrow it will spread its body over this sky.
It will be a day beyond belief.
Tomorrow the sun's face on the snowcapped peak
will be like dahlias in a crystal vase.
That is not a rainbow you see
stretched over the pure, moist, blue,
it is a gate of light.
The rays of light from behind the clouds:
maybe it is the messiah passing through?
What is this? It is hope. It is joy,
and not a hallucination.
Thrill and happiness fill every breath
I inhale or exhale.
In the kindly eyes of friends
there is a green meadow in which joy
is strewn like flowers and confetti at a wedding.
In the garden of my heart faith has bloomed.
It is the morning of our Lord,
without arrogance or deception.

_____

From *Resurrection*, 1973, 61–62.

Mind Blister

If ever I opened a window to look outside,
it was, alas, to a bare wall.
I thought I would make my way to the house of the sun,
but the tunnel I dug opened to the night's dungeon.
My inkpot is a fountain of blood
I have extracted from the blister of an ailing mind.
As much as I tried to say something,
I filled space with nothing but sighs.
When my wings of resolve were untied,
I was free but I could not fly.
It was as if a corpse had been unshackled.
Since I opened my eyes,
it has been to futile repetitions:
night and day, night and day,
my flesh rotting away.
Being born is to begin playing host to death:
it has all been useless talk
for me trying to deny this.
Whether it has been hard or easy,
my eyes have been forced to acknowledge
this being born and dying.

From *Resurrection*, 1973, 47–48.

Dialogue

You said, I will kiss you.
I said, please.
You said, what if someone sees us?
I said, I will deny it.
You said, what if by bad luck my rival walks in?
I said, I'll use my charms to get rid of him.
You said, what if the wine's bitterness disagrees with my palate?
I said, with my lips' nectar I will improve it.
You said, tell me what you see in the mirror of my eyes?
I said, myself, naked.
You said your heart is so impatient,
it wishes to pillage and plunder.
I said, I will treat plunderers with consideration.
You said, to be united with me
you are willing to pay with your life.
I said, I will give you a better deal.
You said, what if one day I told you, go away?
I said, I will procrastinate for a hundred years.
You said, what if I unshackled my ankles
from the chain of your love?
I said, you well know I will find someone
more insane than you.

From *Resurrection*, 1973, 43–44.

Limestone Branches

Oh, I am useless, good for nothing.
Oh, I am fallen, like someone sick.
I grow, night and day,
downward like limestone branches
from a cave's ceiling.
Finding the bones of the dead
in a burning desert is a cause for despair.
The vultures inspecting my body
found nothing.
They beat their wings with anger,
shook their beaks with rage.
I am empty, emptier than sleep,
emptier than silence—
O you, overflowing with life's abundance.
My friends are mannequins, made of clay,
my enemies bloodthirsty wolves and jackals.
My days, my weeks, my years—what are they
but an old tale full of repetitions and mimicry?
O you who have gazed upon a green landscape,
cry out, that you may hear me answer
from behind these walls.

From *Resurrection*, 1973, 41–42.

"Ours"—An Image

Our desires are like a ball,
at the beck and call of other people's feet;
our hopes, a toy in someone else's game;
our victories, no longer fraught with danger,
such as we faced at the gates of Babylon,
but of winning shots and penetrating nets
under the supervision of referees,
blowing their whistles;
our ecstasies, bound by the frame
of a surface that manufactures images,
sometimes of shaking buttocks,
sometimes of shaking heads and breast;
our poems, made for sale at the bazaar;
our songs and music, merchandise
to make profit for merchants;
our blood, stagnant water in a ditch;
our thoughts, putrid blood
in the bodies of the self-indulgent.
Our dreams, gold and silver coins,
glittering like sequins,
their empty interpretations,
joy for the credulous.

....
.......................*

These are the times when
the guardians of honor, name and shame
are the moneychanger and the strongbox.

From *Resurrection*, 1973, 39–40.
*Blank lines in the original censored or deleted [trans.].

Opium of False Promises

The night opened like a black tulip in the sky
concealing crimes and secrets.
The sun, that circle of yellow wax,
melted on the horizon.
In front of my terror-stricken eyes
darkness stretched its hands from every corner.
Cradles yawned like tired mouths,
empty of longed-for children.
A deep pain raged in my heart
for which false promises became opium.
What spirit possessed me
to transform my pure and ethereal contentment
into a rapacious demon?
What made the well-content Eve of my temperament
be tempted by a sheaf of wheat?*
Once I was a cypress free, but now I am like a vine,
begging hands from head to toe.
Now, I sell my prayer rug for a table cloth,
and a bread crust has become my prayer stone.

From *Resurrection*, 1973, 31–32.

*The forbidden fruit of the tree of paradise is apple *or* wheat in certain Islamic traditions (Mojibur Rahman, *Allusions and References in Persian Poetry*, Calcutta, 1974), 109 [trans.].

My Little World

When silver rules, when gold is God,
when the lie is the measure of all events,
when the air we need to breathe and live
becomes a lid suffocating hundreds of voices,
when we wag our tails in frenzy waiting for a bone,
when the smell of food from a neighbor's table
makes your mind and brain lose control
and change into a stomach,
when under the sun men of reptilian constitution
change colors, again and again,
when the womb of honor gives birth
only to prostitutes and coarse men—
in this enormous cesspool of despair
let my world shrink to the point of seclusion.

From *Resurrection*, 1973, 21–22.

The Last Leaf

It hangs on to life by a death-infested hope—
the last leaf hanging from a sycamore branch.
The tender blossoms, their heads bowed, their bodies shriveled—
who has hanged them from the scaffold?
To escape harm a cluster of grapes has taken refuge
in a tomb, hanging from its ceiling like a lamp.
The gutters have suspended ice lanterns on the path,
to help winter find its way to the garden's cemetery.
The almond tree wears resin earrings,
like a poor person who covets the finer things.
The sky has broken the sun's golden carriage
and hung its wheels in a dusty place.
A warm teardrop hangs from the tip of my lashes
waiting to be shed, trembling with anticipation.
The garden is in ruins and Simin has wrapped
the vines of her thoughts around the poplar
of hopes for a new Spring.

From *Resurrection*, 1973, 19–20.

The Rabbit's Garnet Eyes

I will die from thirst.
There is no water in this desert.
These shimmering glass-like waves are but a mirage.
The smiles on these masks hide tears.
These joys are nothing but a mask-made illusion.
I see nothing but darkness within darkness,
mountains of darkness, and beyond this darkness no sun.
Those who make their living off the dead,
reciting verses for a piece of halvah* and bread,
have no efficacious prayers.
The heavy heels of time remain firmly dug in my chest,
and the hands of the clock are in no hurry to move.
Tell the golden-hoofed does,
no velvet grasses remain in this meadow.
The garnet-eyed rabbit cannot sleep
for fear of tigers in these mountains.
Our fancy-ridden heads suffer from a hangover,
but our parched lips have no wine to cure it.
The hailstones falling from the black clouds
have shattered all the lamp-like tulips.
O Simin, the echo of your cry
is your only answer.
For she who speaks to the mountain,
there is no other answer.

From *Resurrection*, 1973, 9–10.
*Sweetmeat or paste distributed to commemorate the dead.

Green Blood

O cursed bird,
my ears ache from your complaints.
O burden,
my shoulders are tired of your weight.
O horror, running through my blood and soul,
I hear your footsteps in every heartbeat.
O flower stalk, accustomed to the snow,
what hope do you have of ever flowering,
while life's green blood remains frozen in your veins?
O never-ending drought,
O barrenness of the gardens of the soul,
not a tulip has opened
since my breast became your wasteland.
You are the horrifying nightmare,
the dream that makes one go mad.
I am devoured every night
by your world that creates pain.
And if ever a smile appears on my face,
acting desirable or desirous,
I am slapped in the face by your demonic rage.
I am worn down by your tyranny.
My poems are bound by your chains.
Your speaking captive has given up speech.
She has abandoned all hope or desire.
She is a stone in the shape of a woman,
the barren woman who shares your bed.

From *Marble*, 1963, 101–2.

Ignorance

O heart, I have spent a lifetime in ignorance.
I have spent a lifetime in self-ignorance.

I behaved like a madman for a lifetime,
but like a flame the end I found was darkness and cold.

Alas, I never came to wear the golden crown of a narcissus.
Mine was the lot of the tulip: a heart bleeding for a lifetime.*

My heart flitted from place to place like a sparrow.
What did it accomplish with this wandering for a lifetime?

Who took my heart? Whose heart did I take?
Whose passion made me act demented for a lifetime?

A handsome face would make me lose my tranquility.
Becoming a connoisseur was the reward for my pains for a lifetime.

I never found my heart and body united.
Every instant I gave my heart to someone
and my body to someone else for a lifetime.

From *Marble*, 1963, 77–78.

*A symbol for many Iranians of martyrdom, elevated sixteen years after this poem was published to the status of a national emblem on the national flag [trans.].

Wine of Light

The stars have closed their eyes, come.
The wine of light flows through the veins of the night, come.
I have poured so many tears waiting in the night's lap,
that twilight has blossomed and the morning has bloomed, come.
In my mind's sky your memory etches lines of gold
like a shooting star, come.
I've sat so long with the night telling my tale of woe
that the night and I have turned pale with sorrow, come.
If you are waiting to see me again when I die,
understand, this is the time, come.
If I hear anyone's footsteps, I imagine they are yours,
with all this beating, my heart is bursting out my breast, come.
You didn't come when the sky was full of stars like grapes,
now that dawn has picked them one by one, come.

You're the hope in the heart of Simin-the-broken-hearted,
put an end to my misery, come.

From *Marble*, 1963, 15–16.

Rival

She stayed awake till the morning,
hatred gnawing at every particle of her being,
a hatred running through her veins like molten lead.

Like a nimble snake, she crept softly out of her bed,
to where that other woman was sleeping
in her husband's warm embrace.

Whispering to herself, she remembered the days
when her husband, her glittering gem,
was not possessed by this demon.

Oh, there was a time when this man sleeping snugly
in the arms of this troublesome woman had a place for *me* in his arms.
Those were happier, warmer days.

It is hard living with the enemy under the same roof
of the same small dark cottage when her heart is radiant with love
and yours is unhappy and sad.

All the charms I used to bring her to shame were useless,
but the charms she used on me were beyond the counteracting powers
of anyone's prayers.

My child was sick, but his father bought sweets and candies for this woman.
It was hard for me bearing the bracelets and clothes
he gave her.

O what nights, when the two of them, drunk and happy
would laugh at my envious tears, as their bodies softly intertwined
like vines in my presence.

From *Candelabrum*, 1991 [1957], 153–57.

She gazed a while at her rival's face, with eyes full of hatred like flames.
In the darkness her own angry face was like a copper sheet
covered with green rust.

With hands trembling she reached for the water
and poured a colorless powder in the bowl, as beads of clear hot sweat
rolled down her face of a bloodthirsty demon.

Tonight without pity or vacillation I must finish off one of these two.
Either I will end up with a husband and no rival,
or with a wretched rival without a husband.

She returned quietly to her bed,
covered her head under the blanket and listened intently,
with her eyes closed, to every sound.

An hour went by. Then, it seemed, someone reached for the bowl.
Her soul leaped out of her body as it lay in her bed.
Her shameless heart began to shake.

She opened her eyes to discover who had chosen
the robe of death and oblivion. Her husband and rival she found still
   asleep.
It was her child who had drunk from the bowl.

She jumped like burning rue and quickly drank what remained.
She threw her child on her back and ran out screaming,
revealing the horror in her heart.

O people, a mother has killed her child! Pity her weeping eyes.
My child has drunk a terrible poison.
Do something. Maybe you can save him . . .

Nightmare

I left my body like smoke rising from a fire,
happy with the thought that I was breaking out of prison.

I looked back at my body. It was calm, cold, lying in bed,
its face tired, its eyes still moist from a not long receding pain.

Through a crack in the door I clutched at the night,
my soul trembling in the phantom-bearing nocturnal silence.

I flew in the dark, gaily, restlessly, at times accompanying
the moaning of the owls, at times, the untimely crowing cock.

On a caravan of breezes I flew through the heart of the city,
till I found my lover in a room sleeping. I gazed at him.

There he was, my shameless, selfish, lover, sleeping,
his chaos-causing eyes hidden under those long, seductive lashes.

I cried out, so calmly sleeping, you, O man with a heart of stone:
may the grave be your bed, may the dirt fill your black eyes!

Wrenched from deep sleep, he leaped from his bed like burning rue,
with fear-crazed eyes searching for me in every direction.

What are you looking for, I asked. This is me: bloody vengeance,
come to wrap my hands around your throat like the shadow of death.

I have come to run my cold ghostly fingers through your night-black hair.
I have come to brand death on your lips with these deadly invisible lips.

He screamed, O phantom, O nightmare, take pity, accept my repentance!
I answered, pity for you who have no pity? Never! Never! Die! Die!

From *Footprints*, 1956, 187–91.

He threw a marble candlestick in the direction of my voice,
trying to make my invisible body shatter and disintegrate.

I laughed with such horror as to make all hues of life flee his face.
He screamed a heart-piercing, liver-slashing, life-extinguishing scream.

His tired body collapsed on the floor, surrounded by the dark and silent
  night.
I listened. He had stopped breathing. His heart had stopped beating.

Through a crack in the door I clutched at the night,
my soul trembling in the phantom-bearing nocturnal silence.

I flew towards my den. It was dark. There was no moon.
I tried to reenter my body. As hard as I tried, there was no way back.

Tombstone

O lost from my heart, my side, my mind,
don't look at me, I can't bear your eyes,
don't look at me, your black eyes evoke
only bitterness and sorrow.

O lost from my heart, tell me the truth,
why have you returned with my memories tonight?
If it's for the one who stole your heart,
I'm not her. She is dead. I'm her shadow.

I'm not her. My heart is dark and cold.
Hers was mad, on fire with love.
Wherever she was, with whomever, in whatever state,
she yearned for you, O unkind idol.

I'm not her. My eyes are silent.
In her eyes were hidden so many conversations.
The sad love in those night-colored narcissi
held more secrets than the night.

I am not her. A smile has not blossomed
on my lips from your love for a long time.
But on her lips a life-giving smile lingered always,
like moonlight on a flower covered with dew.

Don't look at me. I cannot bear your eyes.
The one you want from me, I swear is dead.
She dwelt in my body, then suddenly I ceased to know
what she saw, what she did, where she went, and why she died.

I am her tomb, her tomb. I have covered her warm flesh
with the cold and sadness of camphor.
She is dead, and in my breast this loveless heart is a stone
I've placed at the tomb's head.

From *Footprints*, 1956, 137–39.

Inheritance

Calm down, my child, calm down.
End this childish gaiety and boundless oblivion to pain.
Look at my body withering in pain.

Calm down, my child, calm down.
My heart is heavy. I am restless, bewildered, mad,
mourning the death of true friends.*

Sit by me for a while today.
Put your head on my chest.
Hold me tight in your arms so small and tender.

If your mother cries, stroke her gently,
and look into her eyes with your searching eyes,
that you may understand her secret.

O dear child, on such a day
the pages were ripped from the book of love
and thrown in a fire of hatred and rage.

O dear child, on such a day
so many blossoms of love and hope withered,
so many were carried by the wind to an unmarked grave.

On this sad, sad day
not even a cloud sheds a tear on their graves,
not even a breeze carries their fragrance.

From *Footprints*, 1956, 89–91.

*The time the poem refers to is that of the execution of the first group of twelve officers after the 1953 coup [author and trans.].

You don't know, dear child,
how hard it is to bear this pain:
it is killing me and I can't moan.
My lips are sewn. What else can I do?

The hate you see in my eyes,
take it for safekeeping in your heart.
Of my worldly possessions this is your inheritance. Guard it well!

Dead Man's Tooth

Shivering, scared, uncertain,
he gazed at the cold and fearful grave.
The spark of greed had set his soul on fire.
His mind burned with a hundred flames.

On every grave, rock, and tombstone
the night had spread its darkness and melancholy,
with no sounds to hear but ghosts whispering
and the cries of nightbirds.

He was repeating to himself softly
the corpse-washer's strange words:
"The dead man had gold teeth.
I could see them, when I was washing him.

With my own eyes I saw in his mouth
the glittering of several golden teeth.
But, too bad, I could not lay my hands on them.
I was worried about the relatives."

There he was, him and the treasure
hidden in the mouth
of a cold lifeless body in the grave,
in his hands a cure for all his pains.

If he could get at the gold,
he would change it for money,
with which he would buy for his child
the services of a doctor and medicine.

What good is gold buried in a grave,
useless to anyone:
gold here and an ill person there,
dying for the lack of care?

He struck the grave with the pickax.
The silence of the night crumbled like a wall.
Fear clawed at his soul.
Sweat dripped from his pale face.

Agitated as he was, he kept on
bringing down the pickax, blow after blow.
It was not he anymore digging that night
in that narrow grave: it was his greed.

A spark jumped from his coveting eyes
as the wooden coffin became visible.
His heart beat faster in that dark night
craving for gold.

It was not him anymore, but his greed,
overcoming his fears and weakness.
He tore open the shroud with a stiff finger
and mercilessly pulled out the dead man's skull.

It was a head with a dried-up, cold mouth
full of gold, yes, pure gold,
gold he was offering his soul for,
even if it meant withstanding a hundred agonies.

It was not him anymore, but his greed
opening cold-bloodedly the corpse's mouth
and struggled to extract the gold
from the foul, repulsive gums.

Early in the morning, he took it to the goldsmith.
"Look at this: how much is it worth?"
Testing it, the goldsmith told him with indifference:
"Its yellow color makes you imagine it's gold."

From *Footprints*, 1956, 39–43.

The Prostitute's Song

Pass me the rouge,
so I can add some color to my colorlessness.
Pass me the ointment,
so I may revive my face withered from sorrow.

Pass me the perfume,
to give my flowing hair the scent of musk.
Pass me that tight fitting dress,
so people may hold me tighter in their embrace.

Pass me that see-through shawl,
to make my nakedness twice as enticing in its folds,
to add to the allure of my breasts
and legs.

Pass me that cup of wine,
so I may laugh at my misfortunes in my drunkenness,
so I may mask my sorrows
with a gay and appealing face.

How tiresome he was, how repulsive,
my companion last night.
But when he asked me, I told him,
I had never seen a man as handsome.

From *Footprints*, 1956, 21–24. The same character reappears 40 years later to speak again in her own voice while being buried alive at her own funeral, in Behbahani's short story, "Lay the Stone Gently," in *What Did I Purchase with My Heart: Selection of Stories and Remembrances* (Los Angeles: Ketab, 1996). The biographical short story with a fantastical twist points to a historical character as the basis for the character in this poem: Banu Mahvash, once-prostitute, popular singer and dancer, alleged author of a book of sexual advice, *Secrets of Sexual Satisfaction*, whose funeral procession was attended by the thousands [trans.].

And that partner of a few nights past,
the one who gave me the disease,
even if he paid me a hundred times more,
it would not pay for the pain he gave me.

I know many people, yet I have no one,
no one to stand by me, share my sorrows.
Many make displays of affection,
but they never last beyond the instant.

I have no husband or mate
to grant me their loyalty and devotion,
nor a child to wipe the rust
of sorrows from my heart.

Oh, who is it knocking at the door?
It is my husband for the night.
O sorrows, let go of my heart.
Now we must make him happy.

Lips, lips, cunning lips,
draw a veil of mystery on my sorrows,
so they will give me a few more coins.
Smile, kiss, enchant!

Afterword

Translating Simin Behbahani

Kaveh Safa

Translatability

Translatability is not a function of ease, how close a poem is to a train table, to pure information, that can maintain its purity as it passes from person to person, tongue to tongue.[1] It is rather, as Malkom Khan (in Karimi-Hakkak 1995, 48) and Walter Benjamin (1992, 71–73, 75, 82) saw it, a function of a richness and abundance that comes through, again and again, not only in its original but alien settings. It is the function of a richness and abundance that can not only withstand the trials and tribulations of passage and metamorphosis between languages, literary traditions, cultures, and histories but find in these necessary breakdowns and reconstructions new possibilities to "cast its spell." Translatability is a testament to the ultimate inability of real and figurative walls (censorship, internal exile, political boundaries, war, willed and inherited misunderstandings) to mute the tappings on the wall, to stop the urgent music and messages from passing through. This is why the translators of these roughly hundred Persian poems chose to translate Simin Behbahani and her poems: not merely because they love her works; and certainly not because of the easiness of her poetry, even in Persian (as the poet herself admits as much[2]); but because of its immanent translatability.

---

1. I wish to thank my partner-in-translation, Farzaneh Milani, without whose enthusiasms, encouragement, and work in translating and writing about Behbahani's poetry (Milani 1992, 234–39; 1993, 37–62; 1997) these translations would not have come to be nor this report and reflections about them. I also wish to thank Rena Franklin for her reading of this essay and for her many useful comments and criticisms.

2. In an interview with Farzaneh Milani, 8 May 1998, unpublished manuscript in Persian. The "difficulties" she refers to concern literary and cultural allusions, use of metaphors and oblique forms of expression, and problems in translating beauty.

Afterword

This is not to say from its very outset that the translators of these poems have not been conscious of the "utopian" nature of their project—as, in fact, Ortega y Gasset points out, any translation is ultimately an imperfectly realizable wish (1992, 97). From the outset we have felt the despair of committing linguistic and poetic mutilation, despite our love and respect for Simin Behbahani and her poetry, despite subscribing to an ethos of "fidelity" in translation, despite our "bending" of tools and techniques towards the original and willingly submitting to its constraints ("walking the line," as Rabassa calls it [1987, 83]). We have come to realize the inevitability and sometimes necessity (involving choices we have had to make between limited alternatives) of "things lost in translation."

Since such losses cannot be read backwards from the finished translations and since some readers may wish to have a sense of what they are missing (but cannot gain that sense without familiarity with Persian and Persian literature), the translators thought it might be useful if they point out a few things they consider to have been particularly important but lost in these translations and also discuss some of the critical choices they have made in dealing with the poetry, choices and techniques that have affected the ultimate meanings and forms of the poems—if not always or exactly as intended.

Lost in Translation

Skeletal Music

To the ears of the translators—and ears are not only the poet's major tool but that of the translator, who has to cultivate a sense of "double-hearing" (Rabassa 1987, 82), hearing a poem simultaneously in two languages, in multiple literary and cultural idioms, shaped by different habits, expectations, concerns, preoccupations—the most drastic loss in their translations has been the original music and rhythms of Behbahani's poems and their meaningful shapes, what the poet herself has called their "geometry" (Sadr-eddin-e Elahi 1997), in particular, the music and rhythms and shapes of her ghazals.

While Simin Behbahani is a prolific poet (13 vols., 1951–96) and has worked in many genres—rhyming couplets, ballad-like narratives, unrhymed free verse, script-like poems with scenic descriptions and authorial interjections and "dialogues" in the vernacular, short-stories, critical and biographical-autobiographical essays—the ghazal has been her chosen genre, the genre in which she has most distinguished herself and left her mark. But it has also been the genre most difficult to travel, most difficult to wrench from its original linguistic and literary landscape without losing the most distinctive of its features for Persian ears: a familiar, quickly recognizable exoskeleton, on the constraints and possibilities of which so much of a poem's beauty and meanings depend; and what Simin Behbahani has done with it.

The inherited exoskeleton or manifest form is recognizable by its roughly ten to fifteen thematically self-contained lines, bound by a single rhyme, with every half line metrically equivalent to another, in a sequence of aa, ca, ba rhymes, with meters chosen from a limited set conventionally associated with the ghazal (Fesharaki 1993, 67–82). To these bones are attached, also by convention, a certain amount of thematic flesh, concerns with love or the beloved expressed in a masculine voice but not unusually by a masculine author (Dehkhoda 1960, no. 62, 207; Milani 1997, 9–10).

What Simin Behbahani has done with this inherited skeleton and flesh is, on the one hand, to "make strange" (Ejxenbaum 1971, 13–14) certain aspects of it. For example, while maintaining the ghazal's familiar geometry—its overall rhyme scheme, its metrically balanced hemistiches—she has opened the repertoire of its constituting meters to potentially unlimited improvisation and variation. To her, as with some musicians for whom there are no false notes or rhythms as such, there are no a priori false or right meters: what matters is where you go with a segment of music, rhythm, or speech; what matters is where and when you place it and the relationships you create for it. In Simin Behbahani's remaking of the ghazal, any phrase or utterance may do, whatever its origin (including the vernacular, the language of every day life), to seed a distinctive pattern or structure through echoes and repetitions. The result is striking given the rigidity of the conventional skeleton: in Behbahani's hands it is put together from "found meters." The potential for metrical experimentation and innovation finds its only constraints in the "natural" constraints of every day speech—and in the potential for even the new meters the poet has crafted in her new ghazals to become routinized, not consciously or intentionally repeated by the poet and perceived as familiar by her readers (cf. the poet's own critical reflections on her craft [Behbahani 1993, 175]).

Thematic Flesh

Thematically, too, Simin Behbahani "makes strange" the familiar ghazal by throwing open its gates to themes unfamiliar in their range and directness of expression. The problem this poses for the translators is less losses in "transposition" and "transmutation" between languages and literatures (Jakobson 1992, 151; Paz 1992, 60) than in conveying a sense of the generic tension, renewal, and innovation in Simin Behbahani's remakings of the ghazal.

To be sure, much can be said—even of a philosophical, theological, and political nature[3]—within the idiomatic confines of the conventional ghazal through its talk of love and the beloved, of the real or metaphorical, of female or ambiguous gender, with or without association to real or metaphorical wine, taverns, temples, magis, guides, serving wenches, and intoxication. And certainly many of Simin Behbahani's ghazals are "about" love and the beloved, sometimes ecstatically ("Wine of Light"), sometimes in despair, dealing with themes of separation ("I Write, I Cross Out"), loss ("Tombstone"), confinement ("Green Blood"), disillusionment ("I Want a Cup of Sin"). But there is a difference in magnitude in the sheer range of what her poems can be "about" and in the ways she has used to express them, choosing ways that are not oblique and symbolic but unabashedly and fearlessly direct.

There are few other contemporary Persian poets, including those who have thought themselves liberated from the formal constraints of traditional Persian poetry, for whom we could claim, as we would for Simin Behbahani, that nothing in the poet's world and times seems to have been alien to her poetry.

Thus we would find in her poems philosophical meditations on time, mind, memory, and history ("Lead Insulation," "Mind: Smoke Rings," "Time, It Is Dream Time") as well as talk about the price of eggs on a food line during the war ("From the Street [1]"). We would find sensuous-ecstatic celebrations of nature (the Spring in "Sounds of Blossoms") as well somber talk of fear ("When the Hand of Darkness"), repression ("It's Time to Mow the Flowers"), war ("Raining Death"), revolution ("I Can't Look"), fratricide ("O, Child of Today"), cruelty ("Laws of Lead"), corruption ("My Little World"), censorship ("In My Necessary Silence"), lies ("Don't Read"), exile ("You Leave, I'll Stay"), greed ("Metamorphosis"), utopian blindness ("Opium of False Promises"), hypocrisy ("Our Tears Are Sweet"), disillusionment ("Ears, Ears of Gold"). We would find her talking about her local attachments, to her homeland, people, culture ("You Leave, I'll Stay'"), and certainly religion (Qoranic quotations, allusions, characters, and stories pervade her poems) as well as conveying her sense of being at home in the world, enough to assimilate in her art the rhythms of the Blue Danube ("Whirl, Whirl, My Friend"), His Master's Voice logo ("His Master's Voice"), the Morse Code ("Morse"), Caduceus ("Caduceus"), Buddha (four last poems in *Plains of Arzhan*), Jesus and characters from *Les Miserables* ("I'm an

---

3. It was not merely for writing a love poem that Hafiz, the ultimate master of the ghazal, was charged at various points in his life with apostasy and sedition, with risks to life and limb (Akhavan-Sales 1970, 338–39).

Old Sanctuary"). We would find her patriotic ("My Country, I Will Build You Again") as well as mocking the artificiality and arbitrariness of dividing humanity into East and West ("The World Is Shaped Like a Sphere"). We would find her telling scenes and lives of others: a desperate father turned grave-robber digging for a gold tooth ("Dead Man's Tooth"), a prostitute waiting for a knock on the door[4] ("The Prostitute's Song"), a mother who murders her son by mistake instead of her rival ("Rival"), a mad mother who cannot accept the death of her soldier-son ("Necklace"), an inconsolable one-legged young veteran of the war ("The Man with a Missing Leg"). But we would also hear her in an unabashed autobiographical voice trying to come to terms with the facts of her life, including loneliness, aging, self-doubts—all the more striking, given the codes of modesty and silence Iranian culture and literature prescribe for women. We would even hear her meditating in a self-mocking, melancholic tone on her voluntary submission to the surgeon's scalpel to regain the face of her youth ("I Gave My Face to the Scalpel"). Of course, this is only a thematic selection, but it is enough to bring breathlessness to a Persian reader who might come to her poems expecting to find the familiar.[5]

---

4. In a biographical short story, "Lay the Stone Gently," told from the point of view of the popular and singer-dancer, Banu Mahvash, at her own funeral, being buried alive, the ex-prostitute refers to this poem, "The Prostitute's Song," by Behbahani as her defense and vindication and to the fact that forty years later the poet will not be offended by her name being associated with that of the singer as a writer—referring to a popular, pornographic, book of sexual advice, *Secrets of Sexual Satisfaction*, published under Mahvash's name (Behbahani 1996, 225–45).

5. This is not to suggest that Behbahani is the first or only Iranian poet to "open" traditional verse forms to nontraditional themes more in tune with the times. Karimi-Hakkak in his discussion of the modernist movement in Persian poetry (1995) points out emblematic works by poets such as Dehkhoda, Iraj Mirza, Aref, Lahuti, Eshqi, Bahar, Eʾtessami, in which traditional forms, including the qasideh and ghazal (e.g., Dehkhoda's "Remember," Aref's "Message of Freedom") were adapted to modernist concerns and preoccupations—nationalism, patriotism, constitutionalism, political and cultural enlightenment, progress, social and economic justice, status of women (1995, chaps. 2–5). Behbahani stands out against this background, and from later modernists who sought a further liberation of relevant-contemporary content from archaic forms, for the range and scope of her thematic opening. Whether by temperament, such as her combination of encyclopedic "interests" with intellectual, artistic, and political independence; or whether by circumstance, as in her longevity, her survival against the odds for an Iranian woman poet (Milani 1997, 6), hence her ability to realize potentials denied to Eʾtessami and Frrokhzad by their early deaths (at thirty-four and thirty-two, respectively)—Behbahani seems to

She violates generic-thematic expectations; not only of the traditional ghazal but also in much of contemporary Persian poetry, which may be confined thematically less by manifest generic prescriptions than by the emotional, intellectual, and ideological predilections of individual poets and the times; not only by what she says in her works, by her thematic breath, but by how she says them. Here we are talking less about music and "geometry" than about range of directness/indirectness in expression. A Persian reader may not only be shocked by the nakedness of her autobiographical voice but also by the clarity and detail of the mirror her poems hold to her times, including its major traumas of repression, revolution, and war.

The mirror the reader is used to has a reflecting surface covered with patches of symbolic fog that diffuse light, create a "soft focus," even when reflecting the horrifying and the grotesque. The reader is likely to be accustomed to a penchant (whether by force of habit, choice, or circumstance) even among self-consciously modernist poets for oblique, symbolic, and abstract expression: for skewered nightingales standing for silenced and censored poets; for dogs giving up their freedom for a piece of bone and

---

have bucked the trend following the thematic opening of Persian poetry (in traditional or "new" forms) of closing it again with a new set of formulaic concerns and figures. She has avoided closing it with a narrowly defined set of ideas and sentiments about social, political, and cultural "relevance" or "commitment." These are ideas and sentiments at the center of which is not unusually the figure of the poet as a guide or voice of the people; the poet as a witness to the times; the poet as a prophet, often angry for being unheeded. These are ideas and sentiments dominated by a master-narrative: of a neo-Manichean battle between "light" and "dark"; between good and evil; between lies and false consciousness and the truth; between the oppressed masses and local and foreign tyrants. These are ideas and sentiments structured by a mono-myth or paradigmatic allegory that, however symbolically disguised (for example in the language of birds, dogs, wolves, or fishes), always tells the same story, always can be deciphered by the same "keys." Examples of this can be found in Nima Yushij's apocalyptic revolutionary bird poem "The Amin Bird" and its allegorical interpretation by the poet Kasra'i, both discussed in detail by Karimi-Hakkak (1995, 262–72). Of course, there are exceptions to this tendency, notably, in works by E'tesami, Farrokhzad, Sepehri. While Behbahani's thematic concerns overlap theirs—including Sepehri's painterly-ecstatic naturalism, Farrokhzad's autobiographical reflexivity, E'tessami's irony and philosophical play with the politics of everyday life—her poems cast a much wider net: covering a much wider range of experiences and concerns in life and art: from war to plastic surgery, ghazal aesthetics to public flogging, smell of coffee to philosophy of time, Qoranic verses to conversations in a food-line.

shelter standing for moral and political compromise; for ornithology to pro-vide prophets and emblems of doom and change; and for meteorology (ubiquitous dark clouds, stormy nights, dawns and sunsets) to function as barometer of the political, moral, and cultural climate.[6]

The contrast Simin Behbahani provides is not absolute. She too can express herself in the oblique and symbolic mode: resort to a little black fish that grew and grew to tell the story of an emerging tyranny; resort to the patient camel to meditate on a people's threshold of endurance, being able to take so much and no more; resort to the snake-shouldered king of Iranian epics and mythology to protest the dangerous political and cultural games which allow make-believe snakes turn into real ones. But she can and has also done something else.

There is no soft focus as she protests the times when school children are executed by firing squads ("Twelve Fountains of Blood"); when child war-riors are identified by the remains of their body parts ("O Child of Today"); when crippled young veterans are too full of rage for motherly consolation ("The Man with a Missing Leg"); when mad mothers oblivious to the world walk the streets carrying the ghosts of their dead sons ("Necklace"); when moral righteousness means enthusiastic crowds stoning a woman to death, and progress means finishing her off with a cement block ("From the Street [6]"). There is no disguising of the poet's voice here, of her anguish and out-rage against the cruelties of revolution even when just ("I Can't Look") and against war even if imposed. Her voice is all the more striking in its naked-ness given the time of its utterance: the enthusiasms of a just victorious rev-olution and the throes of a seemingly endless war, not the best of times for exercising one's freedom of expression.

The fact remains, however, that Simin Behbahani and her audacious poetic tongue have survived over a half-century of Iranian politics and cul-ture that has often made writers pay dearly for such audacity (for a recent list of such payments, see Simin Behbahani's "Interrupted Speech," 1997, in this volume). There is no simple explanation for this achievement—the very need for explaining such an achievement, a long, productive *and* out-

---

6. For example, Shamlu's "nightingale kabob" (1980, 30); Akhavan-e Sales's "The Dogs and the Wolves" and "The Rabid Wolf" (1956, 78–84; 122–25); Yushij's "Statue Bird," "The Amen Bird," "Phoenix" (1963, 87–88, 89–91, 55–63). Few contemporary Persian poets—and presumably readers—find it easy to resist meteorological symbolism as a "short cut," like background music in certain films, to establish personal and/or collective mood, tone, attitude, diffuse meaning, interpretation, and commentary. The examples seem to be every where, from "serious" to popular poetry.

spoken literary life, is symptomatic of a political and cultural landscape that seems to demand especially from its women writers an early and tragic death (Milani 1997, 6). Among the things such explanations would have to consider would be aspects of her personality that have contributed towards her being a "survivor," "fighter," enduring and resourceful in the arena; her beliefs and commitments, which have always been too expansive to suffer the confinements of a political party and its credo; and the various contingencies of her life and time—all beyond our purview here. What may be relevant here—even if only as speculation—is how her art itself, in which she has given prominence to the ghazal, has contributed to her survival by camouflaging its potentially "dangerous" content, at least in the eyes of adversaries too blinded by generic expectations: that with the ghazal's recognizable geometry can only come the timeless talk of love and the beloved, the temple and the tavern, the guide and the serving wench, spiritual or material intoxication; that the self-contained, independent lines of the ghazal are far too disconnected to sustain a politically dangerous thought or argument; that the aura of archaism surrounding the idiom as well as the form of the ghazal make it emotionally and intellectually too fuzzy to make real contact with the consequential issues of the time.

By violating these expectations Simin Behbahani may have revolutionized the ghazal, but by maintaining its recognizable form she has been able to express feelings and thoughts that may have otherwise been too quickly recognized and suppressed as revolutionary.

We close this discussion of thematic remaking by emphasizing its formal aspect: that not only has the music of the ghazal a distinctive shape upon which Simin Behbahani has left her mark by her metrical innovations; but thematically too the ghazal has a shape that Simin Behbahani has radically transformed. We are referring here to the thematic autonomy of lines (two metrically equivalent hemistiches separated by a space, or sometimes written as two lines), each line expressing a complete thought or feeling, without any necessary connection to the line above or below—of course with the possibility of a deep resonance or structure connecting these manifestly disparate parts. Simin Behbahani has made manifest this structure, thematically shaping many of her ghazals in the form of a narrative, or drama, or philosophical meditation, or argument, with aesthetic and rhetorical punch-lines. This may be a loss for new found American fans of the traditional ghazal, attracted to the strange mixture in it of a rigid musical form and surrealistic thematic "discontinuity," "unexpected juxtapositions" or "jumping" between parts (cf. Doty 1996). But for the Persian ghazal and Simin Behbahani it has meant a less restricted opening to the world, a significant renewal.

Afterword

Friction

There is a sense of tension and excitement in Simin's ghazals between the received and the new, between generic conventions and "deformations" (Tynjanov 1971, 72–73), between the commonplace and the poet's uncommon reworking of them (Ortega y Gasset's "doxa"/"paradoxa" (1992, 101) that is lost in translation, irrevocably. No amount of syntactical, idiomatic, and formal literalism, supplemented by a phonemic transcription and footnotes "reaching up like a skyscraper" (Nabokov 1992, 127) can recover the experienced and crafted embeddedness of the translated texts; the sparks and heat generated by their friction against other texts; their interaction with a multiplicity of literary, linguistic, and cultural contexts, many of which may be unconscious or semiconscious to the poet and her readers, and none of which may be exhaustively described.

Of course, there may be tensions and excitements in the translation but from another uniquely complex embedding, from other intertextual, generic, linguistic, and cultural frictions. Even if analogies could be found between the two sets, they are likely to be trivial at best (if not purely "theoretical" rather than aesthetically experienced) or "accidental" at worst, infusing through partial analogies radically different sets of meanings and feelings, aesthetic effects.

Thus a translation of a Simin Behbahani ghazal that tries to imitate the shape of its music and rhythm in English, producing a poem with monorhymed lines and metrically equivalent hemistiches and, contrary to the effect produced by the form in Persian (an easy if deceptive familiarity), would foreground in English a sense of the exotic or archaic, against a backdrop of free verse as the familiar and conventional.

On the other hand, in translating Behbahani's ghazals into free verse in English, we have come to realize, with a mixture of consternation and astonishment, another kind of accidental effect: a sense of the translations reverberating backwards on the originals, "hearing" them as if they were written by someone else, in a different musical key, with different set of frictions distinguishing their embeddedness. To choose between these two kinds of metamorphosis has been the dilemma faced by these translators. Our guiding principle, if not always realized, has been to choose the one that least "blocks" the original light (Benjamin 1992, 80) in Simin Behbahani's poems; to choose the metamorphosis that seems more to realize a possibility inherent in the original than a negation of it—in the vein, for example, of "what if Simin Behbahani had chosen free verse as her metier, without the formal constraints and possibilities of the ghazal?"

Texture

If poetry is food for the heart and the mind and the imagination, an important aspect of "style" that distinguishes a group of poems or a poet's works from others is "texture": their smoothness or "crunchiness" to our linguistic, aesthetic, and interpretive palate; how quickly or with what resistance they yield their tastes and nourishment, how "difficult" they are, how much "effort" they require for this purpose. In this respect, too, Simin Behbahani's poems have suffered a major loss in translation: a measure of "difficulty" that distinguishes most of her works.

It isn't that Simin Behbahani has not written poems that are relatively easy to digest: with relatively uncomplicated vocabulary and syntax, with transparent figures and rhetoric, and with quickly recognizable ideas and feelings, brought to play in the frame of a quickly recognizable story, argument, meditation. Such were, for example, her early ballad-like stories "Dead Man's Tooth" (1953) and "Rival" (1963), stories with a clear social message about poverty (and the monsters it can make of good men) and polygyny (the monsters it can make of loving wives and mothers), told in a style in which a Poe-esque sense of the grotesque, irony, and pathos is mixed with a De Sica-like "neo-realism" for maximum melodramatic effect. And such have been later poems, such as her "Wine of Light" (1963), for all its simplicity, as moving and hypnotic an invocation of the beloved (every line ending with an irresistible, *bia, bia,* "come," "come") as to be found in any ghazal; and her series of "From the Street" poems (1983–85), for all their incorporation of every day speech, scenes, and concerns (for example, in a food line, discussing the price of eggs) as evocative as any documentary film (in fact, some poems incorporate a film-script format) on life under conditions of a seemingly interminable war.

But many of her poems convey a greater sense of crafted "difficulty," a crunchiness or granularity in their diction, syntax, reference, and symbolism, requiring deliberation and work by the reader.

Diction

While she may share with modernist Persian poets an opening of poetic diction to the language of the vernacular, to colloquialisms, to popular and local expressions—for example, have two women standing in line for rations ("From the Street [3]") discuss the commotion around them by resorting to oxymoronic slang, "flying elephants" (why all this commotion? as if . . .) and "pulling a hair off a bear" (meaning: it is as difficult to come by anything in these hard times, as it is to extract a hair from a bear)—Behbahani also shares with modernist Persian poets a penchant for thickening the literary texture of her expressions, for giving them a gravity and resistance usually not found in everyday speech.

Consider her diction, for example. She may use archaisms, such as *gazmeh* (in "Necklace") rather than more common and contemporary words for armed guard or policeman; similarly *yamin* and *yasar* rather than the familiar *rast* and *chap*, right and left ("The World Is Shaped Like a Sphere"). She may use rare words such as *hudaj* rather than more common and everyday equivalents for chariot *(arrabeh, kaleskeh)*. She may use a manifestly "literary" chariot, *garduneh*, rather than a more mundane equivalent for motorcar (sent by the government), in her dream-like scenes of air raid blackouts and mass arrests ("When the Hand of Darkness"). She may choose the manifestly literary *Gosalandan* over the more ordinary expression for tearing, *pareh-kardan* ("Nightmare"); similarly, *tirazheh*, a term unlikely to be encountered in everyday speech, over *qows-o-qazah*, the more familiar term for rainbow ("Song [4]"). She may mix the abstract and the concrete to make the latter strangely palpable, as in *bagh-e tarikh* (the garden of history), and use an unusual idiom for any Persian poetry, *qey*, "vomit"/ "nausea," to add horror to that palpability—induced by eating blindly a grape from the vine of history, which turns out to be an eyeball ("You Said, It's Only Grapes").

She may use "specialized," thickly Arabified Persian (the language of law and the clergy) for satirical purpose, as in *shar'eh anvar zad sala*, or "the illuminator of the laws summoned" (the believers to a stoning, in "From the Street [6]"); or she may use a pair of purely Persian words, *palid palayad* ("purify the polluted") rare in their alliterative combination, for literary effect ("Oh, I made love!"). She may resort to neologism, create new words from familiar components. For example, in *siman-sar shodan*, being (literally) "cemented" (hit by, as in a public execution, not "shoed" or encased by cement as the neologism might mean in American English), she coins a more "fitting" word to suit the times, the progress from the age of death-by-stoning to death-by-the-cement block ("From the Street [6]").

Or she may even put foreign words to good use in her poems, like T. S. Eliot but without footnotes: as in "His Master's Voice," the English title of a poem in its original Latin alphabets, "about" memory, nostalgia, her childhood, her mother, an old gramophone, records, needles and grooves, and the dog on the record's logo; or in a poem called "Morse" in English, "about" news from the war-front with critical comments "heard" in the pecking sounds of a Persian woodpecker; or in a poem titled, simply, "Caduceus," "about" a world so ailing that even its emblem of healing is not well, its wings broken, its stick dried up, its snakes shriveled.

Afterword

Persian readers attuned to the music of her poetry may also be more attuned to the "motives" (in the linguistic or aesthetic sense) underlying the "difficulties" she introduces to the language of her poems by her choice of words and new coinages. They might sense the poetic pull towards "literariness," seemingly irresistible for traditionalist and modernist poets alike (with some notable exceptions, such as Farrokhzad and Sepehri), against the background of the gulf that separates spoken and written, formal and informal Persian—much wider than it is in English. They might also sense the constraints on her choice and molding of expressions by the form of her new ghazal, its demands of monorhyme and balanced meters. For example, her unusual designation of certain ants as plunderer(ing) red ants, *muran-e sorkheh yaghmayi,* may seem more "necessary," even if *qarat-gar* may be a more common and understandable choice for plunderer(ing) than *yaghmayi,* once we take note of its place in a sequence of half- and full-line end rhymes beginning "The Ants' Leftover": *maqzi, nimeh-gerduyi, niruyi, andisheh-ha-yeh sodayi, muran-e sorkh-e yaghmayi, har-suyi* (respectively: a brain, a half a walnut, a power, mad thoughts, plundering red ants, every which way).

Syntax

The thickening of linguistic texture perceived in Behbahani's poems may also be the result of her play with Persian syntax, involving inversions, omissions, contractions, complex concatenations, which may not violate rules of Persian grammar but subject every day usage to a "literary" strain. To discuss these manipulations in any detail is beyond our purview here, especially since it would require conveying a sense of "base line" as well as its licensed literary violations. It suffices to point out that Behbahani's play with syntax is not unique. It is shared by many poets, traditional and modern. It may elicit more work from the reader, like mirror reading or filling in omissions, which becomes less disorienting as the reader becomes attuned to the literariness of the language at hand and the style of the particular poet. Behbahani's poems in this regard, for all the tautness and complexity of their language, are less disorienting than those of many other contemporary Iranian poets. The constraints imposed by their musical "geometry," with their manifest, palpable order, tend to make clear, disambiguate potential ambiguities in the reworked syntax of the poetry.

Reference

But as if not more important than diction or syntax in crafting "difficulty" into her poems are Behbahani's infusions of cultural, historical, and literary references and representations in her poems—major reasons why she herself thinks her poems are difficult too (written interview with Milani, 8

May 1997). The scope of what her poems are "about" is encyclopedic, unlike any other contemporary Iranian poet, and requires a corresponding engagement of the heart and mind and soul of the reader, which sometimes can be hard work, even if pleasurable.

A sense of this scope should have been conveyed in our earlier discussion of Behbahani's thematic opening of the ghazal. Here it may be more useful to consider this scope from a close-up rather than panoramic angle: to consider not the variety of classes of things she refers to and represents in her poems but the variety within one such class. Take Persian poetry for example. Even if we consider just one book, *A Trajectory of Speed and Fire*, a collection of ghazals written between 1973 and 1981, and even if we limit our examples to merely explicit references, such as dedications, epigraphs, quotations, invocations, addresses, dialogues, and comments—we find this class of references to be encyclopedic in itself.

She certainly is not the modernist ideologue who has self-consciously turned a blind eye and deaf ear to her literary ancestors. They speak to her and through her to her times. Thus we find Saʾdi (d. 1291), cautioning the poet who in a dark night of the soul, overflowing with despair and rage, is contemplating to use her poems like matches to start a hundred fires: "don't play with fire / if your house is made of reeds" (in "I Sell Souls"). We find half a line of Rumi (d. 1273), ". . . What I cannot have I desire," resonating in her poem, "I Want a Cup of Sin," in which utopian desire turns into a nightmare, in which playing God and creating the new Adam ends with creating a monster, who will, like Frankenstein's monster, torment his creator.

Neither is she the traditionalist poet who looks down at her modernist contemporaries, even those who have embraced "free verse." We find her dedicating a poem to the poet Akhavan Sales, quoting him, footnoting him, even incorporating the "hope" (*omid*) in his pen name (M. Omid), in a bleak poem "about" moral and political impotence ("In the Deep Blue Sky"). We find her dedicating a poem to the memory of the poet Sohrab Sepehri, addressing the dead poet with a juxtaposition of his own ecstatic, sensual, natural, images (extensively footnoted) and images he would be forced to witness had he lived, images of war and fratricide ("Your Death Is Death of Quickness" [as in the images of flowing water in his poetry]). We find her dedicate, "O Love" to the poet Fereydoon Moshiri; and begin "The Velvet of Dark Lashes" with an epigraphic quotation from the poet A. Sayeh. In "Laws of Lead," we find her weaving in through a quoted hemistich, "I tear at the stars," a multi-layered segment of poetry from Manuchehr Atashi, to express her feelings of inconsequentiality, vulnerability, and confinement. In that segment one poet's cry of despair is already interwoven with those of another poet, Masʾud Saʾd (d. 1137), a prisoner for fifteen years in India, and that of the Biblical Benjamin (Ibn-e Yamin), falsely accused, imprisoned, and held hostage in Egypt; and the unhappy state of the three (with Behbahani's, an implicit fourth), is given further dramatic impact by evoking the image of another poet, Hafiz (d. 1389): what the prisoner yearns for is not Hafiz's immortality, celebrated in song and dance, but a mere opening to the sky. And on a lighter note, we find her writing a farewell poem to the poet Nader Naderpoor, "You Are Going Away, Happy Flying," borrowing the image of the light-and-quick gazelle from one of his poems ("In the Manner of the Gazelle") to complement him and his poetry.

This interweaving of other literary voices and figures and segments in Behbahani's poems is all the more remarkable for being interspersed in the same book with references to, and poetic engagements with, real and consequential historical events: including a poem written on the night of the infamous Black Friday (7 Sept. 1978), when government troops opened fire on demonstrators at Jaleh Square ("What a Cold and Somber Silence"); a poem written on the occasion of a massive newspaper strike the same year, when it was rumored that to collect the bodies of the dead, one had to pay for the bullets that had killed them ("On the Leather Table Cloth, Tonight . . ."); and shortly after, poems on the unwanted war ("We Didn't Want It, But It Is There"), its destruction of real cities and people (on the occasion of Khorram-shahr, literally the City of Joy, turning to Khunin-Shahr, the Bloody City, in "Write, Write, Write," dedicated to its defenders) and the terrible things it does to children, not only to their bodies but souls ("O Children of Today").

But should you imagine that with these literary and historical references you have figured out the circumference of the world of her poetic preoccupations, she will surprise you with a botanical soliloquy ("Green Cypress, Teacher of Patience"), proving how good plants can be to think and feel with, that a little known plant, *shang*, "edible desert plant," too can deserve a footnote, or she will surprise you with a meditation on sunsets, Salomeh, and historical necessity (in "The Wind Proclaims the Victory of Sunset").

Of course, these are samplings of only one book. Undoubtedly the texture of her references to and engagement with the world (real and imaginary) has only thickened in the course of her long and prolific career (thirteen books published by 1996).

Symbolism

Should the reader bring to Behbahani's poems a sense of the world commensurate in breadth and complexity to the world of her references—not an effortless task in their original setting, even more difficult in translation—she or he will have to deal with another difficulty: what the bits and pieces of the world are made to "mean" in her poems. For, even if things in a poem convey meanings and feelings recognizable from experiences outside the poem—a pre-condition for their use in a poem—rarely do they convey *just* that, and not something more or less or even different.

Even the seemingly transparent quotations from real life conversations in the "In the Street" poems, in their assimilation in the music, geometry, drama, rhetoric, and moral-political "intentions" of the poems, become something different. The poems may "elevate" a simple conversation on a food line (about the price of eggs, milk, cigarettes) to an exemplar, a "symptom" of the times, quoted with irony, anger, despair, and/or gallows humor (the woman who has just given birth in the line, without skipping a beat, demanding double rations). They may elevate the fates of particular men-at-war, men mutilated, broken down, forgotten, to pathos-evoking archetypes, drawing on the connotations of their names: Biblical Joseph, "not [yet] eaten by the wolves," Abbas (symbol of Shiʾa heroism, valor and self-sacrifice at the Battle of Karbela) broken down, Qodrat (literally, "power") crippled, house-stricken. Or they may "demote" with irony and dark humor otherwise significant life-events such as death and burial ("pressures" to be experienced within the grave "taught" and rehearsed by bodies pressing against each other in a food line) or giving birth (also in line, a pretext for casually asking for double rations), such deflations of significance making them sad commentaries on their times.

Such transformations of references (already linguistically and culturally meaningful) into symbols in a poem (with a second order of meaningfulness, shaped by the poem) may exude a greater sense of opaqueness or ambiguity to the reader: of idiosyncrasies that fascinate but resist a quick reading, and of multiple meanings which resist a quick interpretation.

Take for example her use of "natural" or somatic references. They often play the role in her poems of "ritual symbols" (Turner 1970, 28–29), fusing subject and object, concrete and abstract, the sensual and the ideational, moral, spiritual, social, and political, but a fusion not always serving the same poetic or rhetorical purpose.

Clearly, in some of her poems, body parts, fluids, processes, and sensations are put to the use of making more palpable—whether grotesquely, pathetically, matter-of-factly, ironically, or ecstatically—a wide range of feelings and ideas.

Take the eyes, sight, tears, for example. In "I Can't Look," an eyeball extracted from its socket like "the swamp bubbles . . . emptied of all joy and sadness," like a stone extracted from a ring, makes grotesquely palpable the author's revulsion at the relish with which the newly victorious regime displayed the tortured and bullet-ridden bodies of powerful men of the old regime, however responsible they may have been for its evils, after their arrests, summary trials, and executions. This is not the kind of "justice" the author had in mind in her opposition to the old regime. In "You Said, It's Only Grapes," the reader is compelled to taste blindly with the author the fruit of the vineyard that is history, to find that "it tasted of vomit and blood," to find that it is a crushed eyeball. In "The Necklace," a mad mother, mad because of the death of her son at war, oblivious to herself and the world, also has had the two grapes of her eyes plucked and "squeezed by the times to fill a hundred barrels of blood." In "Raining Death," written during the war (1985), the author's complains about the newly arrived Spring, not because of the "natural" turbulence it brings, in the mode of "The Waste Land" ("Memory and desire, stirring / Dull roots with spring rain,") but because her eyes cannot see through the horrors of war, "you are green again, why can't I see you? / You're visible, and I have eyes, why can't I see you?" For her this is a spring, "blood-scented, demented." Two years later (1987) tears have become "sweet" to the palate and laughter "venomous," with doubts difficult to dispel about the prospects of peace: about sewing back together "wings and heads" pulled from bodies," wondering if they will come back to life, ever fly?

Heart, breasts, and blood too are used in many poems to intensify meanings and feelings. In "Twelve Fountains of Blood," idyllic images of freshness, innocence and youth, running water, jasmine braids, and breasts like buds clash with the horror of the poet finding one of her young students executed, the number twelve of the twelve fountains signifying the clip of twelve bullets in semiautomatic guns at the time emptied in her breast. In the poem "O Child of Today" the poet protests the bloodshed and ethos of war, the futility of "wash[ing] out blood stains with blood."

But the focus of these images can also be more personal; for example, they can be about writing or love. We find in "Mind Blister" another "fountain of blood," this time used to express her feelings of confinement in writing. In this poem the fountain of blood is her "inkpot," its contents what she has extracted from the "blister" of her "afflicted mind." And blood can also be "green," associated with life, fecundity, Spring, but "frozen" in a loveless marriage in which the poet turns into a stone in her husband's bed ("Green Blood"). In a more upbeat poem, ecstatically about love, of the kind celebrated by Rumi, in which I and not-I become indistinguishable, not only is the poet filled with the Spring, the sounds of its "blossoms opening inside her like the Pleiades, / singing, 'it's me, it's me,'" but her veins turn into the strings of an instrument she plucks singing and hearing herself ("Sounds of Blossoms"). In another poem, "Love Came So Red," we hear the poet celebrating once more love but in darker tones, mixed with a sense of confinement, barrenness, and coming too late. The love that "came late" in this poem is all the more breathtaking for growing like "a red flower growing in the snow"; for the poet expressing her despair about her heart being too "swollen . . . for its cocoon"; for her heart wishing to "fly" though its wings "have rotted in their confinement." And in a poem about longing, separation and loss, the heart is a "thorned fruit" hanging from a plane tree ("Thorned Fruit"), reminding us of another heart, turned into a "porcupine . . . taken . . . refuge in [her] breast, / wearing out [her] body with its spines and restlessness," in "Mind: Smoke Rings."

References to other body parts, womb, skin, brain, bones, and limbs, contribute similarly in many of her other poems, making ideas and feelings more intensely palpable. This is what she achieves in her "Ants' Leftover": evoking a state of mind through images of "frenzied thoughts" as red ants attacking her brain split open in her skull like a walnut. In "Dry, Lifeless, Dry" she expresses her anguish at the barrenness and aridity of the times (1980), with the "master" screaming "musts and must nots" everywhere, by evoking images of a dry womb: "Dry, lifeless, dry. / Devotion dry. Womb dry. / Such dryness and sterility / cannot give birth to even something dry." In an earlier poem (1973, heyday of the Pahlavi regime), it is not such barrenness she protests but "the womb of honor giv[ing] birth / only to prostitutes and coarse men," befitting a time "when silver rules, when gold is God, / [and] the lie is the measure of all events" ("My Little World"). But then, the womb can also be "filled with light," embody hopes of salvation ("Maybe It Is the Messiah"), or embody the poet's sense of ecstatic poetic fecundity: "My poems and wild mint bear messages and perfumes. / Don't let them create a riot with their wild singing" ("It's Time to Mow the Flowers").

In some poems it is limbs tied up, shriveled, amputated that make palpable a sense of personal or collective confinement and impotence ("I know something must be done, / but not by someone with her hands tied like me," in "Morse"), or mindless cruelty ("We pulled wings and heads from bodies" then having a change of mind, tried to sew them back together, in "Our Tears Are Sweet").

In some it is bones. It is bones used in an inversion of the *dance macabre* to evoke the imperturbable stillness and quiet of a shrine-cemetery at night, where you can't hear a "moan or a murmur or a hum" or "a dead man drumming on a skull with his shin." Or it is bones used to evoke the poet's sense of unrelinquishable attachments to her homeland and culture: "Till my last day you will hear in my bones / the same "tale of the reed" (a line finishing with "complaining of separations" in the opening lines quoted from Rumi's Mathnavi, in "You Leave, I'll Stay," in which the poet explains her rejection of voluntary exile).

In some it is the face and skin. It is the face the poet has given to the surgeon's scalpel, at the risk of pain and life, to regain the beauty of her youth, but she meditates self-mockingly in her poem about the futility of her wish and the shortcomings of the surgeon's blade to change not her face but heart: the block of ice it had become into flowing water; the "pathetic," "decrepit" cat into a "mighty lion" (in "I Gave My Face to the Scalpel"). It is the skin that conveys a sense of elemental vulnerability: in the symbolically charged obscurity and oppression of a cave, something cold and wet slithering up her skin: "oh . . . oh . . . a snake, I think!" (in "A Bat or Some Other Creature"). It is the skin that may be shed, emptied, like a snake's to convey the sense of fright and anxiety during nights of blackout and mass arrests: "I could see my body lying in bed, / emptied, abandoned, / as if a snake had extracted itself / from my lifeless skin" (in "When the Hand of Darkness"). Or it may be the skin the poet wishes to shed like a snake: "to flee from my self in a shining body" (in "Oh, I Made Love!").

However, as in her poetic meditation on plastic surgery, there are poems in which somatic references are less symbolic means—making sensually palpable potentially more distant and abstract ideas and sentiments—than ends, with their significance closer to the fate and experiences of the body. Thus, a fever can be a fever, a "flying" and "falling" pulse the symptoms of a real child dying (in "It Was the Pulse Flying"), and not figurative expressions for mystical religious experience, a tempting interpretation the translators had to forgo on advice from the poet (more on this later). And the "restless" heart may be "calmed" not by the elixir extracted from the slashed skin of metaphorical poppies, but real ones prescribed by the physician (in "Heart, You Are So Restless").

Animals too, as we have just seen with the case of snakes, are made to carry a heavy burden of meaning and feeling in many of Behbahani's poems. What is not obvious to the reader of the poems only in translation is the extent to which these uses—and others, of botanical, astronomical, and technological figures—achieve their aesthetic or rhetorical effect by going *with* the grain of literary and cultural conventions or *against* it, by repeating the familiar and/or elaborating it in less familiar directions.

For example, the camel in "And Behold" (one of the most popular of Behbahani's poems, in high demand in poetry recitations inside and outside Iran) "works" so well clearly because of the familiarity of its signifying burden, like somatic symbolism making palpable the idea of patience (political, economic, moral) that has reached its limit, endurance about to give in to murderous rage. Similarly *in the grain* are many of Behbahani's birds: through their bound and broken wings ("Mind Blister" and "Our Tears Are Sweet"); through their plucked feathers ("In My Necessary Silence"); through their vulnerability to assault ("The Ants' Leftover"); through their confinement in a cage ("Enough in This Old Land"); through their meaningful onomatopoetic or "coded" utterances (the *haq haq* of the *haq haq* bird demanding "truth/justice" in "Gypsiesque (15)" and the pecking of the woodpecker delivering "needed" messages in Morse code from the war front in "Morse"); and through their free flight ("In My Necessary Silence") serve as palpable representations of the self as person and group, the self as it is (often bound, confined) and/or what it could or wishes to be (free).

However *in the grain* representations may be elaborated in unfamiliar ways, adding to their impact. For example, in "Fossil," even if birds are put to familiar use to express the poet's melancholic sense of confinement juxtaposed with wished-for freedom, they are made to carry the idea of confinement to its imaginative extreme: not by broken wing or cage, but by being reduced to a petrified trace in a rock. The self in this poem is stone-bound: its only possibility of movement is if some living bird lands on it. Similarly, very familiar conventional snakes, probably the best known in Iranian literature and culture, make their appearance in "I Used to Tell You." But here the brain-devouring snakes growing out of the shoulders of the evil king Zahhak are presented with a narrative twist which brings them much closer home, as not merely the afflictions of a demonic "alien" being, but a potential in everyman, including "loved ones" close to the poet. In games begin responsibilities, warns the poet: make-believe snakes can turn into real snakes, make-believe tyrants into real tyrants. In the poem her warning is unheeded; she goes on being "frightened" by "games that end in massacres." Her nightmare, with palpable analogies in contemporary Iranian history, is fulfilled: "Now snakes do not frighten me as much as the loved one."

In some poems this sense of moral and political foreboding is all the more provocatively expressed for going *against the grain* of conventional uses of zoomorphic symbols: by explicitly dissociating the familiar from their familiar meanings or feelings. Thus in "Ears, Ears of Gold" (1982), the little black fish," intrinsically endearing for being small (vulnerable) and black, and made even more endearing by Samad Behrangi's (d. 1968) political fairy tale for children and grown-ups, *The Little Black Fish* (a revolutionary fish that challenges the status quo, the tyranny of fish-eating predators and the "false consciousness" and resignation to their fate of other fish, making it to the ocean through heroic acts of courage, endurance, and wit, "organizing" other little fishes on the way) is shown to be capable of a very different kind of metamorphosis. The poem presents the post-success story of the little black fish, now a living symbol of ruling ideas and powers: "a leviathan / of mountainous size, its mouth gaping like the mouth of hell to swallow the sun." However, the poet takes one step further against the grain by rejecting a solution that mimics the origins in violence and intolerance of these dreams turning into political and cultural nightmares. Just as she cannot condone the cruel punishments (torture, mutilations, executions) meted out to representatives of the previous regime, bloody though their hands may have been (in "I Can't Look"), she is unwilling to "kill in anger" the angry and venomous snake that has "coiled itself by [her] side." For it is "domestic" (in "If the Snake Is Domestic").

Plants too find similar uses in Behbahani's poems.

In some it is an idiosyncrasy of associations that enhances their meaningful palpability: for example, an onion, with its layers of skin, standing for a prison designed like a Chinese box, with "walls that enclose me" ("O Box Within Box"); a walnut split open like a walnut standing for the brain under attack by "frenzied thoughts" like red ants ("The Ants' Leftover"); the night "opened like a black tulip in the sky / concealing crimes and secrets" (in "Opium of False Promises"); or "Two Rows of Acacia Leaves," in their "order," "harmony," "balance," tranquility, unity, and camaraderie, the opposite of the poet's self-mocking characterization of herself and her relationships.

In some poems it is the familiarity of conventional figures that produces meaningful palpability. For example, in "Can You Really Fly?" written on the occasion of a first batch of political prisoners being freed in 1978, a tough, wizened, maple tree "standing tall by the crossroad, / learning from a thousand calamities" is made to embody the character and attributes of an old fighter, selfless and resilient. In the melancholic, winter-struck "garden in ruins" of her poem "The Last Leaf," "hope" (for a new Spring) is a poplar tree around which the poet "has wrapped the vines of her thoughts." But most conventional of all, so evocative a symbol as to become a national emblem on the flag of the Islamic Republic (displacing the old lion and the sun), is the blood-colored "tulip," symbol of suffering and martyrdom, used by the poet in 1963, to meditate on her state of being, her "lot" (in "Oblivion").

In some poems it is the elaboration or play with conventional meanings and feelings associated with plants that produces their "special effects" in the poems. Not only can Behbahini's readers in Persian recognize in her poems a culturally given "language of flowers"—and for that matter, of "trees" and "gardens" and "vegetation"—but they also appreciate the author's idiolect.

Take the lily, for example, and Behbahani's use of chromatic variation— sometimes verging on the imaginary—to set and shift *tones* in a poem and / or to evoke different constellations of meanings. In one poem "A Lily, Like a Smoke Ring," four differently colored lilies set the progressively darken-ing tones of the first four stanzas. "A lily, like a smoke ring: dark, blue" sets the mood and "stirs" the world of the first stanza: cries rising from river-bank, from the extremities of sleep, from the foundations of haste: "arise!" "whose is it?" "hurry!" A lily "like a crimson flame, / . . . a contest of smoke and fire" sets the tone and introduces us to the world as a garden in flames in the second stanza. In the third an encompassing sense of confinement, helplessness, spreading fear, and death is introduced by "A lily, cold as fear, yellow as death." Darkness and barrenness rule in the fourth stanza, intro-duced by "A Lily like a black snake, coiled around the moon." In a fifth stanza, the poet shifts the accumulating darkness of the poem by enjoin-ing the reader to "Plant a white lily with the face of the sun," so that "light" may spread "across the plains," so that the "day open[ed] its pores to good fortune." In another poem, "O Box Within Box," the white lily comes to epitomize the author's wish for liberation: to one day break through the onion-like prison of walls within walls and "praise God like an iris in the mountains."

We should stress, however, that for her readers in Persian the symbolic efficacy of trees, flowers, grains, grasses, nuts, fruits, and their ensembles as gardens lies in their providing not only *means* to think and feel about other things but functioning in certain respects as *ends* in themselves, *as if* their value was inherent in them, so deeply rooted in literary conventions and Iranian culture as to seem self-evident, natural. (This is the culture that conceptualized paradise-*pardis*, the ultimate good life, as a garden, and in significant ways still does.) This seemingly inherent significance is at its most palpable in poems that evoke images of its violations, often to lament the terrible times or attack it with satire and irony: hence the image of the burning garden in "A Lily, Like a Smoke Ring," or, even more terrible, of the gardener setting fire to the garden (in "I Swear on the Fig, and I Swear on the Olive"); hence the reproach, "We have been like children, beyond any account or accounting / We have broken every stalk like a wild wind in the garden" (in "Our Tears Are Sweet"); hence the lamentation about the times (war, black outs, night arrests) when the only music heard in the garden is the groaning of old crows, when old "death-worshipping ghosts" so fill the air as not to leave room for the jasmine and lily to breathe (in "When the Hand of Darkness"); hence the poet's sarcastic invitation to the "enemies of Spring" not to forget her, not to "spare" her, as they "mow" the flowers, "stomp" on the grass, chop down the elm, cut the branches off the maple, since her "heart is greener than green, / flowers sprout from the mud and water of [her] being" (in "It's Time to Mow the Flowers").

Behbahani's poems convey a sense of intensity of attachment to plant life that is not merely "given" by literary convention and cultural predilection. It seems to be a personal attachment that manifests itself in her language of plants. Against the stylistic grain of many of her literary cohorts who seem to have a predilection for describing things as if "seen by moonlight" (to borrow a figure from Rebecca West), in their outlines, generic forms, not particularity or details, for Behbahani flowers are rarely merely flowers; they are lilies (and their different kinds), tulips, jasmines, narcissuses . . . ; trees for her are poplars, oaks, elms, cypresses. There is even room in her poems for an occasional botanical footnote, such as on *shang*—"an edible vegetable found in the wild"—which she compares to *shanbalid*, fenugreek, the one in Spring being as good as the other in Winter (In "Green Cypress, Teacher of Patience").

Like plants and animals, celestial figures are put to use in Behbahani's poems sometimes "in the grain"; for example, the familiar use of the Pleiades in "Sounds of Blossoms" as a flower or a blossom (a close cluster of stars, like petals making up a flower), both botanical and celestial symbols used to convey a sense of ecstatic opening of the soul; or the sun, implicitly female, with "orange-tresses," invoked by the poet to minister her badly needed warmth ("When will you melt this dirty snow?") in "The Orange-tressed Sun," with conscious or unconscious kinship with *khorshid-khanum*, lady-sun, evoked in early versions of the Iranian flag, in combination with a fiercely or comically masculine lion (Najmabadi 1995). In other poems the celestial symbols are all the more powerful for their idiosyncratic twist on conventions: for example, the sun in "Opium of False Promises" is not the melter of dirty snow but itself "a circle of yellow wax" melting on the horizon; in the nightmarish poem "You Said, It's Only Grapes," when the make-believe grape picked from the "garden of history" tastes like "vomit and blood" in the poet's mouth (it's an eyeball, she discovers), the world begins to roll like a "millstone" and the stars and the moon were "raining blood"—as evocative an expression of anguish in Persian as "Spring, blood-scented, demented," mentioned earlier.

Human devices, whether artistic or technological, also prove themselves good to think and feel with in her poems.

In a more obvious way they may serve to create an aesthetic distance, hence irony, in describing man-made horrors: for example, describing aerial bombardment in "Raining Death" not by enemy planes but by "iron eagles."

Or familiar "big questions" of authorship and purpose may be raised by fresh images of human manufacture(ing): raising the questions Khayyam asked through images of the potter and the puppeteer in less metaphysical and more palpable social and political terms, through the images of an absent toy-maker's workshop: "These cardboard horsemen mouthing epics on their lips, / whom do they seek to battle? / The medals they wear, these lifeless wooden figures, / of what glories do they boast? / The hearts of the children of this city / waiting to be molded like sculpture's clay, / whose hands do they await to mold them?" (In "Workshop"). Or it may be the hubris of manufacturing the "New Adam"—from a "cup of sin" and "clay mixed with corruption"—that the poet questions through a mixture of Biblical-Qoranic, sensual-sexual, and moral-political allusions. A memorable attribute of this man-made Adam, who like Frankenstein's monster turns on its creator, is an "organ of shame" growing on its forehead. Or it may be the arbitrary but reified divisions of humankind into East(ern) and West(ern) that the poet questions through the use of a globe, the spherical map of the world: "the world is shaped like a sphere / It has no left or right . . . / You can't take your bearings from a globe, / if with the flick of the finger you can make it turn / this way and that." (in "The World Is Shaped Like a Sphere").

Adam is not the only figure with a supernatural aura to enter Behbahani's poems. Others, demonic and sacred, already thick with meanings and sentiments, enter the poems from Iranian (and sometimes non-Iranian) sacred narratives, legends, and folklore. Here, too, the translators wish to point out, they enter the poems in different ways, through less or more significant transformations, some decidedly against the grain of received conventions, a difference that tends to get lost in translation. Two examples of Behbahani's applied demonology may point this out: the different uses of the figure of the *Div* (a monstrous, anthropomorphic personification of evil, physically or supernaturally powerful but "perverse" in its rapacity and antisocial behavior, pre-Islamic in origin but assimilated in Iranian-Islamic folklore and legends) in two equally powerful poems: "Gypsiesque (13)" and "You Won't Believe It."

In the first poem Divs behave *in character:* "as they soar in the sky" and "smoke . . . trails" burning eyes and throats; "plunder[ing]" from the "maidens" "the silk and rubies of their lips and cheeks"; and forcing the maidens to serve them, among other things as cushions for their sleeping heads, "In her lap every maid holds a monster's head / like a piece of firewood set in silver." And in this poem Divs are perceived as they usually are: personifications of greed, power, and oppression, with an additional emphasis here on gender oppression.

In the second poem, a Div conjured up from childhood tales, "the tales my nanny used to tell me," also acts true to form, physically and morally: its angry eyes like "volcanoes," spewing "violet and crimson lava; a greedy "extortionist" bent on stealing from the poet the "unbelievable" treasure she has found in her fists, stars from which light "seeps out" when she squeezes her fists, stars that make the "quicksilver" in her "glass-like bones" glow green. But in its conclusion, after the poet has confronted and destroyed the monster from her childhood beliefs, the poem radically transforms the conventional perception of the Div. There is a dramatic "reversal" and sad, melancholic "recognition": the kinship between the magical stars and the terrifying monster; the willful destruction of childhood's beliefs in one entailing the loss of the other. This is how the poem ends: the poet contemplating her victory, the "fallen" Div" squirming in its own blood," and she opening her fists to find the stars have also vanished.

Finally, let us turn to the people who populate Behbahani's poems, who enter it as already meaningful "types," and consider the metamorphosis some of them undergo as they become symbols in Behbahani's poems, especially metamorphosis *against the grain* of more common literary and nonliterary conventions.

Merely the range of types that find their way into Behbahani's poems runs against the grain: hence the "shock effect" for her readers in Persian to encounter voices and points of view of a prostitute ("The Prostitute's Song"), pickpocket ("The Pickpocket"), grave robber ("Dead Man's Tooth"), humble school teacher ("Teacher and Pupil"), giving accounts of their lives and problems and preoccupations in *Footprints,* her 1956 collection of poems; or, later, the strangeness of encountering in ghazal form and through the poet's undisguised voice, often outraged or in despair ("I Swear on the Fig, I Swear on the Olive"), the tyrants of the day ("I Used to Tell You"), the torturer ("Our Tears Are Sweet"), the executioner ("From the Street [6]"), the zealot ("Dry, Lifeless, Dry"), the warmonger ("Raining Death"), men "who lose their heads fighting for a hat" ("What a Cold and Somber Silence"), the child-soldier ("O Child of Today"), the war-crippled ("A Man with a Missing Leg"), the "graveyard parasite" ("The Rabbit's Garnet Eyes") the mourning teacher ("Twelve Fountains of Blood"), mourning mother ("Necklace"); or encountering the merely quotidian, men and women who stand in food lines ("From the Street" [1] and [3]), who "compromise" themselves every day for a piece of bread ("Metamorphosis," "Our Image"), mothers anguished by their children's privations and spirited children stealing what they desire but cannot have, such as pistachios at inflationary prices ("The Child Followed").

But for many "types" it is not the fact of their incorporation in a poem that runs against the grain but how they are incorporated, or rather, reinterpreted by the poet. To clarify this point, we have to make do with only a few examples: one, the figure of the prophet-seer-savior, of seemingly ubiquitous significance in contemporary Iranian poetry (cf. Ghanoonparvar 1984; Karimi-Hakkak 1995, 262–72); the other, the figure of the gypsy, less familiar in poetry if not life, elevated into a major archetype by Behbahani.

Her interpretations of these figures are distinctly multilayered and complex.

Take the figure of the prophet-savior-seer. On the one hand we find Behbahani dreaming as innocently or fervently about deliverance and deliverance personified in the figure of a prophet-seer-savior-seer as have many other contemporary Iranian poets: for example, the allegorically "disguised" messiahs of Nima Yushij, the "Amen [*Amin*] Bird" and the "Phoenix"; the legendary self-sacrificing savior of ancient Iranians, Siavush Kasrai's "Arash the Bowman"; or the down-to-earth messiah of Forugh Farrokhzad, redistributing Pepsi Cola and social justice in "Someone Who Is Like No One Else." Such is Behbahani's poem, "Maybe It's the Messiah," literally a "vision" of hope, filled with images of illumination, fecundity, purification, joy: including a "horizon" with its "womb filled with light"; friends with eyes filled with joy like "flowers" or "confetti" at a wedding"; a "morning without deceit or arrogance." And such is Behbahani's poem, "Footsteps," in which the deliverer is imagined in more sensual-personal terms: "carry[ing] a torch," passing through the poet's street, distributing "candies and rosewater," giving the street a "different fragrance and hue," to grant perhaps the poet's wish to "tear this curtain of darkness / from this house of sorrow."

But even though the hope for salvation and/or a savior is expressed in many of her other poems, so strongly as to seem a moral-political "commitment," it is often mixed with darker thoughts and sentiments: doubts about its realizability and alarms about its darker potentials "realized" in contemporary Iranian history.

Thus it is not the atmosphere of a wedding that pervades the poem, "A Bat or Some Other Creature," but an atmosphere of doubts, uncertainty, obscurity, confinement, futility, desperation, such as found in the "deep cave." To keep her spirits up and to endure, the poet, surrounded by darkness, by the smell of rot and decay, by menacing unseen predators, puts into songs and slogans her hopes for deliverance, hopes embodied in the figure of "the knight [who] will rise / from the seed in the water" (the three saviors of Zoroastrian eschatology, one for each millennium after Zoroaster, to rise from semen left by Zoroaster in a lake, when the times are right and the appropriate virgins are available for insemination in the water). But the hopes she voices are answered by the monsters and the beasts in the dark, repeating the refrain, "You wait in vain, you wait in vain."

In "Ears, Ears of Gold," it is not doubts that cause despair but a utopian wish realized as a nightmare: the plucky and endearing "Little Black Fish" of Samad Behrangi's revolutionary fairy tale has made it to the ocean (after fighting pelicans and organizing other fishes on the way, becoming a leader and an emblem) to become literally a big fish, a "leviathan of mountainous size: / opening its mouth like the jaws of hell / to swallow the sun and the Eastern sky / in darkness." On a more personal level this is the New Adam wished for and manufactured in "I Want a Cup of Sin," a greedy, concupiscent, tyrant.

What is distinctive in Behbahani's representation of this social and imaginary archetype, in comparison with other contemporary Iranian poets, is its irresolvable tension, ambiguity: simultaneously asserting the necessity[7] of hope for salvation, including its personification in the figure of seers / prophets / saviors (to which we could add guides, leaders, champions, voices of the people), however utopian and beset by doubts; and a relentless, iconoclastic skepticism, readiness to protest false messiahs, manufactured Adams.

On occasion the voice of Behbahani too, like many of her peers in contemporary Iranian poetry (cf. Ghanoonparvar 1984; Karimi-Hakkak 1995, 262–72), merges in her poems with that of the seer/prophet/savior—though more Christ-like, winning hearts by "unbounded charity," as in "I'm an Old Sanctuary," than by the more usual moral and political hectoring of often not sufficiently heeded hence resentful poet-prophets. However, important as this figure may be in Behbahani's poetic meditations on individual and collective hope, it serves less as a figure through and in reference to which the poet defines herself in her poems than that of the gypsy.

Not only is there more of the gypsy in her poems—in sheer quantity, sixteen poems in her collection *Plains of Arzhan* are titled "Gypsiesques," ostensibly dedicated to the figure, while references to the gypsy abound throughout her works—but the gypsy does more for the poet as a complex mirror, as a partner of interior dialogues, and as an emblem for various aspects of Behbahani's identity as a woman and as a poet.

The mirror the gypsy presents is a complex one: both in terms of the "reality" of the gypsy used as a mirror, with living counterparts in Iranian society, and in terms of what concerns and realities of the poet the gypsy is used to voice and represent.

---

7. This "necessity," as if it were a moral and political "commitment" as well as a "foundation" for supporting the world of her heart and mind, is given more generalized expression in terms of having, holding on to, and loosing "beliefs," "convictions." Conviction provides the "feathers and wings" without which the released political prisoner in "Can You Really Fly?" cannot fly. And belief is what the poet despairs of losing: "She who walked, her arms laden with faith, / now suffers by necessity the poverty of her faithlessness" (in "Love Came So Red"); "With doubts settled in the shelter of the eyes, / faith will repudiate truth, / even if it shows its face" (in "Doubts, Doubts, Doubts").

Regarding the first, there may be a core, however amorphous or open to exceptions,[8] of social and historical "reality" in how gypsies are represented in Behbahani's poems: such as physical mobility and women gypsies plying their skills in music, dancing, fortune-telling, dispensing folk remedies for the heart and the body. But nevertheless they remain "stereotypes" in the poems as they are outside, stereotypes of "familiar strangers" (Sway 1988, 4–5) whose strangeness can elicit "projections" and fantasies more "symptomatic" of the state of mind and heart of the user of the stereotype than the reality of real women and men stereotyped. Among the most glaring distortions in this stereotype are: a feminization of the gypsies (whether in literary references or references in everyday speech, of "gypsy" (*kowli/luli*) as a label or attribute almost always referring to a woman, as if there were no gypsy men, or, as if, by implication, gypsy men were less than manly; and, compounding this distortion, the assumption that gypsies as women are less bound by codes of honor and shame that constrain the sexual and social life of other women, that they are less "modest," freer to express themselves in voice, body, and affairs of the heart.

Applying this stereotype implies an obliviousness or turning a blind eye to the possibility that gypsy men may be alive if not particularly well off or well regarded in Iran, engaged in a variety of occupations from farmer (of watermelons in Zargar village, near Qazvin) to tinker, peddler, smith (iron, copper, gold), making drums and flutes and felt tents, carving mouthpieces for the hookah, training, trading, and performing with animals (cf. McDowell 1970, 58–68); and that gypsy women, despite their physical mobility and work that brings them into visible contact with nongypsies (mostly women), may also be subject to the constraints of a fiercely patriarchal society, including male-centered concerns with sexual honor and shame, male-centered taboos controlling female "pollution," modesty codes controlling women's appearance (scarves and long skirts, even before the resurgence of veiling in Iran), physical comportment, and interactions with

---

8. Not all Iranian gypsies are nomadic or work in the "typical" trades associated with them: for example, the goldsmiths-turned farmers growing watermelons in the village of Zar Gar settled there by Nader Shah in the eighteenth century, whose language has been studied by the linguist Don Stilo (McDowell 1970, 164). Similarly, regarding their patterns of settlement: not only may they live in villages, but in urban settings, such as in the Bibi Dokhtar neighborhood of Shiraz, or some may follow transhumant nomadic patterns, such as groups of peddlers, tinkers, or smiths attached to sections of larger tribal-nomadic tribal groups like members of the Qashghai Confederacy (Bahman Begi, in McDowell 1970, 163).

the opposite sex, which not only preclude anything resembling "free love" or promiscuity but romantic love—marriage in this fiercely endogamous society, no less than in the society surrounding it, being largely an affair between families, shaped by individual-transcending economic and political considerations.[9]

Even though Behbahani too uses this stereotype, with its core of reality mixed with distortions, it undergoes a distinctive transformation in her poems: not in content but in how it is valued, significantly affecting the distance presupposed or created by the stereotype between self (nongypsy) and other (gypsy).

She presents an alternative to two major ways the stereotype is commonly used in Iranian life and literature: certainly not as most commonly used in every day speech, in which to call a woman "gypsy" (*kowli*) or label her conduct gypsy-like (*kowli-gari, kowli-bazi*) is an insult, an insult which translates the various "freedoms" (of speech, action, movement) attributed to the gypsy by the stereotype to expressions of "loose" character and morals, as repugnant or dangerous.

Nor does she use it in the way found in some Iranian love poems, in which the negative stereotype is retained along with the distance it presupposes between self and gypsy-other but is found perversely attractive, contributing to an Iranian version of the femme fatale, as for example in the archetypal fusions of the "beloved" and the "gypsy" (*luli*) in Hafiz's ghazals: the "gay, intoxicated, gypsy" in one;[10] "saucy, beguiling, mayhem-making" in another;[11] and a "thief" of the poet's heart, "intoxicating," "promise-breaking, killer, chameleon" in another.[12]

From the first she differs in keeping the stereotype but inverting how it is valued: making virtues of the gypsies' "boundary transgressions," as Milani

---

9. There is very little reason to believe Iranian women gypsies are any less constrained by pollution taboos (*marime*) than are their American or British sisters, for whom not only menstruation and giving birth are polluting to men but so are women's bodies, clothing, underwear, and proximity, e.g., moving in front of a man (Sway 1988, 53–56; Vesey-Fitzgerald 1973, 43–54). Similarly, there is little reason to believe they are less constrained by rules of endogamy and pragmatics of arranged marriages (cf. Sway 1988, 64–67).

10. As in the line "Zephyr, of that gay and drunken gypsy / what news have you, how is she?" (Ghazal 274, line 5, in Hafez 1983).

11. As in the half line "Woe from these saucy, seductive, mayhem-making gypsies" (Ghazal 3, line 3, in Hafez 1983).

12. As in the line "Stolen is my heart by one like a gypsy, intoxicating / promise-breaker, killer, chameleon" (Ghazal 260, line 1, in Hafez 1983).

calls them (1998, 14–15). From the second she differs by taking out the implicit distance (and with it, the social and moral superiority implicit in the distance, however masochistically denied) out of the figure of the femme fatale. She can say as Hafez could not or did not: "I am the gypsy, oh, yes" (in "Gypsiesque [1]").[13]

But this is not a simple identification or idealization. The mirror the gypsy holds up to Behbahani is multilayered: it reflects doubts, alarms, and admonitions as well as wishes for a selfhood thwarted, repressed, or difficult to realize. Rarely is the gypsy merely "described" in Behbahani's poems, with a reality complete and taken for granted. More often she is the subject of prescriptions, proscriptions, and commiserations, in which addresser and addressee are difficult to separate.

Thus even in "Gypsiesque (13)," in which the figure of the gypsy is represented in the most stirringly heroic terms, as if in an anthem or marching song for Iranian women:

Gypsy, stamp your feet.
For your freedom stamp your feet.
To get an answer, send a message with their beat.
To your existence there must be a purpose under heaven.
To draw a spark from these stones, stamp your feet.
Ages dark and ancient have pressed against your body.
Break out of their embrace,
lest you remain a mere trace in a fossil.

Gypsy, to stay alive you must slay silence.
I mean, to pay homage to being, you must sing.

---

13. A major Iranian poet that could, all the more remarkable for being male, is Mehdi Akhavan-e Sales, in his well known poem "Winter," in which he calls himself gypsy-like to convey a sense of homelessness, stigmatization (political in his case), abandonment, betrayal, literally being left out in the cold ("It's me . . . your sad gypsy [one who is like a gypsy]"), and in his poem, "A Fable," in which he uses the contrast between an old and youthful gypsy to represent himself and a former comrade and drinking companion: "I am the old gypsy, reproachful, with a deadened heart / You, the fleet-footed, restless, young gypsy." In a self-consciously more direct line of descent from Hafez's "Drunken Gypsy" as femme fatale is Rasul Parvizi "Drunken Gypsy" in a short story by the same name, in which the author reminiscing about his youth and passage to manhood remembers his "first love," a married adulteress, who dispenses sexual favors for cash, a sexual "pythonness," which he romantically refers to, with a nonironic nod to Hafez, as his "Drunken Gypsy."

The "heroic attributes" associated with the gypsy are not simply assumed but "urged" upon the gypsy, as if urging her to act true to character, to realize the potential in the stereotype, and to overcome the obstacles for this realization. In the same vein, she does not "describe" the gypsy as a self-willed woman who can take care of herself, as the common stereotype would suggest, but urges her to have a will of her own, not to "take it" anymore: "Gypsy you needn't accept everything he says. / Listen to someone else for a change. / Go, if he said 'don't go,' may your feet be swift / Don't come, if he said 'come,' may your ears be hard of hearing. (In "Song [5]")." In the same vein, she urges her not to "cry herself blind" but sometimes to follow the example of the camel, who may appear calm and patient most of the time, but who occasionally gets mad-drunk ("Song [3]")—to "bite through the arteries" of the cruel driver, as she elaborates the image in a later poem ("And Behold"). In the same vein she "reminds" her in "Song (4)": her heart is (ought to be) not only beautiful, but with "Mars as crown and rainbows for wings," a "fighting cock" (in Song 4). By making transparent the wish behind the idealized image of the gypsy (evoked predominantly in the subjunctive and imperative moods rather than the indicative), implying lacks to be filled by the wish, she simultaneously de-reifies a wish-fulfillment fantasy and anchors it in reality (the lacks and the constraints ignored by the stereotype).

Her doubts and hesitations, too, regarding possible outcomes of the wishes fulfilled, intensify this effect. As with her treatment of the figure of the prophet/seer/savior, they bring a utopian ideal down to earth: the gypsies' wishes for freedoms, given the real constraints of Iranian society, also entail "costs" and "punishments"—the consciousness of which when the freedom are voluntarily assumed add a tragic or sacrificial quality to the gypsy as a heroic figure.

Thus, in one poem she may urge the gypsy to express herself freely: "The cry repressed will kill you. Scream! Howl! / . . . / Haven't you muffled your voice long enough? / . . . / Break your wall of silence, / . . . / Tear your heart out of your chest / and smash it on the brow of waiting, / . . . / Climb the rooftop, proclaim it" (in "Gypsiesque [15]"). In another she may pay reluctant homage to the "reality principle": counseling censorship for the protection of heart and limb. She urges the gypsy to "hide [her] heart in the closet"; not to "give [herself] away" with love, but to "burn like a letter unread thrown in the fire." She warns her: "Such unhidden crying will stain your reputation"; that she should put even a mask to shame with her "counterfeit" laughter without cause ("Gypsiesque [14]"). Otherwise, punishments may follow from being shackled and jailed to being stoned ("Gypsiesque [9]").

But she also takes account of the pain and hatred such repression entails: "Centuries of oppression have seeped into your bones, / beyond the powers of time to drain." In these conditions when love appears like the "Spring" settling on the "plains of your soul," it is a "leprous" Spring; "what else fills your ulcerous blossoms / but the pus of hatred," "every flower is a wound / with five bloody petals / every swaying branch a seven-tailed whip" (in "Gypsiesque [14]").

And yet, in a more heroic-tragic mode, she may suggest as costly as the transgressions she urges may be ("Drive away this terrible silence from this house / Sing, dance, and yes, laugh, boisterously"), they may be worth it, even if they entail death by stoning ("Gypsiesque [11]"). Her ultimate gypsy-hero is a *kamikaze* for love: ready to take the poison she carries in her ring, and if that fails, to resort to the dagger in her sleeves. In the "Autumn" of her life, she "knows the punishments for intoxication, but is not afraid." She "would die for love, rather than renounce it" ("Gypsiesque [9]").

The figure of the gypsy, then, is no less ridden with ambiguities—apparent contradictions (Empson 1966, 191–92)—than that of the seer/ savior/ prophet; among these being: the gypsy imagined as some sort of super-woman (in heart, will, tongue, action) *and* as especially vulnerable, deficient in some or all these attributes; the gypsy urged to rise to her heroic potentials *and* cautioned about its costs and punishments; the gypsy imagined as an inevitable victim *and* as a tragic hero. However, overarching all these is another ambiguity, one that holds and weaves the others together, intensifying their meaningfulness, intensifying the dramatic and aesthetic tension in the poems: this is the ambiguity of identity and difference between the poet and her representations of the gypsy.

There are hints in many of the poems—for example, references to age, Autumn love ("Gypsiesques" [9], [12]), sense of exile ("Gypsiesque [8]"), concerns with self-expression and the barriers and sanctions against it ("Gypsiesques" [14], [15])—that in various respects the gypsy addressed or described in these poems is the poet herself, even if wearing the clothes of a conventional stereotype of the "other." In some poems this relationship, or rather, identity, breaks through the surface, with dramatic effect.

Such is the first poem in the series of Gypsiesques. It begins with a conventional distance between the poet (her voice, persona in the poem) and the gypsy, a distance which enables the poet to address the gypsy as a client or supplicant. What she wants from the gypsy, whose powers she evokes ironically (evoking popular superstitions, "what my nanny used to tell me"), is not the usual vague promises of good fortune ("in thirty days, thirty weeks, thirty months"), but the transparently impossible: oracular insight into her beloved's heart (does he love her still, at all); a magical cure (talisman, prayer, special herb) for what ails her heart (loss of beloved to a rival). Even more impossible, she wants the gypsy to take her away to the land of gypsies. Of course, the "weary" poet receives no answer. The gypsy only echoes her demands, as if in mockery. The last four lines of the poem provide a key for understanding this state of affairs: "I am the gypsy, oh, yes. / Here there is no one else but me / The gypsy's image is visible / as long as I face the mirror."

As we realize the addresser and addressee in these poems are by and large one, that who the poet is urging on or cautioning or commiserating with in the poems is mostly herself, that the doubts and affirmations the poems express are not about the state of heart, mind and actions of some other person, the figure of the gypsy also loses the two-dimensionality of a stereotype. Its merger with the poet both "deconstructs" the stereotype and infuses it with the subjectivity not of a distant "other" experienced and defined from the outside but of a "self" viewed and engaged in a dialogue from within. The apparent contradictions in the figure become meaningful as the necessary "incompleteness" or ambiguity (Bakhtin, in Clark and Holquist 1984, 71, 79–80) of a self contemplating and representing itself.

Balancing Choices on a Tightrope

Not all difficulties and losses in translating Behbahani are, as we have discussed them, specific to translating her poetry. Some are generic to the process of translation itself; some a product of choices made by the translators practicing their craft, choices reflecting different goals and expectations, technical and philosophical orientations, attitudes towards and involvement with the materials of their translations (author, work, genre, language, culture). The following are some of the choices we have had to make, choices that we believe have significantly affected the shape and meaning of our translations—of course, it should be understood that not all our choices have been "free," in the sense of being independent of the opportunities and constraints of circumstance, and not all the results of our work have followed our intentions.

One set of choices, bearing on the quality and intensity of contact and exchange in our translations (between languages, poetic traditions, and cultures), has been about labor, how we have divided it or shared it.

While this has been a joint effort—two bilingual translators, with occasional help from the author—it has not been a "team translation" as Guy Daniels calls it. It has not followed the "procedure whereby a non-poet who knows a certain foreign language prepares a prose translation, or crib, of a poem in that language, which is then versified by a poet ignorant of the tongue in question. (Daniels 1987, 170)" Not that remarkable poetry cannot come out of such a procedure—such as the English ghazals of Adrienne Rich and William Stafford based on "literal" translations with linguistic and cultural glosses by Aijaz Ahmad of Ghaleb's ghazals in Urdu (in Ahmad 1971), or Coleman Bark's free but powerful "versions," as he often calls them, of Rumi's *Mathnawis* based on more literal versions by Moyne, Arberry, and Nicholson (Barks 1995). However, "inspired approximations" (Ahmad 1971, vols. 18–19) as they may occasionally be, much of their virtue is "accidental", in the sense of being a product of compounded insensibilities: of the original author to the ultimate shape and meaning of her works in translation; of the "literal translator" to the ultimate destiny of the "raw" materials she or he reproduces to be used in an aesthetic production in an alien tongue; and of the ultimate translator to the embedded music and meanings of the original as an aesthetic object. To the extent that translation involves some kind of mimesis, here it is through a glass very darkly. And however tenuous the contact or resonance between the original and its translation, here it is too quickly cut off: the translation taking on a life of its own, independent of the rhythms, tones, intentions, and preoccupations of the original. With Goethe we could ask, what is the point of translating Ferdowsi, if it is only to "Germanize" him, to make him another German poet? (1992, 61–62)

Of course, the point may be some form of poetic or cultural narcissism: at its most benign, using the other as a mirror, to see more of oneself and better; at its worst, an unabashed cannibalism, using easily digestible bits and pieces of the other for aesthetic or spiritual nourishment or stimulation—in both, the "center of gravity" of style and imagination, literary and cultural concerns being clearly located on native grounds, closest to one's own face, heart, mind, and stomach.

It may be making a virtue out of necessity that we, as bilingual and bicultural translators whose mother-tongue is Persian, have tried to keep the center of gravity of our translations the poems in their original language. We have tried to minimize the "drift" towards narcissism—in part irresistible since all translation involves some degree of assimilating the "strangeness" of one language and aesthetics into the familiar terms of another—by doing three things.

First, we have tried to keep open the thresholds between the houses of language and culture till the very last—almost to the point of publication— by going back again and again to the originals, subjecting our versions to their constraints and influence, not unusually discovering fresh undertones, shades of meaning, discovering "differences that make a difference" (Bateson 1972, 315) in Behbahani's poems and in our translations of them.

Second, given the density (stylistic, semantic, and rhetorical) of Behbahani's poems, the possibilities of multiple interpretations (sometimes simultaneously) they present, and the fact that a translation while choosing some interpretations is likely to eliminate others, and that some of these eliminations may seriously affect the ultimate tone and the meaning of a poem—we have tried to more consciously take account of these changes by systematically comparing the differences in our interpretations, engaging in a sort of "interpretive triangulation," using our different vantage points to more clearly set off a core of distinctive features beyond which the poems cease to be Behbahani's poems.

Third, faced with the most difficult of such problems of interpretation, we have taken advantage of the accessibility and patience of a living author, asking her for help on many an interpretive impasse. Her help has been especially crucial in translating poems which go against the literary grain—such as a penchant among many contemporary Iranian poets for oblique or symbolic modes of expression. Had we, for example, translated "It Was the Pulse Flying" as a figurative description of an ecstatic experience, as one of the translators had initially interpreted the poem, our translation would have meant something quite different than that intended by the poet: a painful meditation on the death of her grandson from leukemia, with the soaring and dipping pulse referring to the soaring and dipping pulse of a dying boy.[14]

Having benefited from the long distance advice and encouragement from the author, especially at moments when making choices among interpretations seemed like walking a tightrope—sometimes in a fog—we feel sorry for literary translators for whom the author they are translating is literally or figuratively dead. We lament the willful acts of literary and linguistic "matricide" (Johnston 1992, 51–52), however "playful" or desperate they may be.

In the fog or not, translating Behbahani has often been for us like walking a tightrope, trying to keep a balance—not always with the same degree of success—between choices, trying not to fall into the chasms of extremes on either side regarding issues such as literalism, fidelity, authenticity, flow.

Take the first issue. We have tried to steer a course between the academic literalism of an Iranian Professor Horrendo—bane of literary translators, so dubbed by Sara Blackburn, who "In his anality . . . fetches his dictionary and finds that on page twenty the translation reads 'chair' where the true

---

14. Clues for such an interpretation are also provided in Behbahani's autobiographical reflections (1996, 181–86).

meaning of the original was 'stool,'" thus guarding in an arbitrary and aesthetically decontextualized manner the "integrity" of the author and the original language (in Rabassa 1987, 82)—and the liberality of "lowelization," dubbed after Robert Lowell by Guy Daniels, for his "anti-translations," "imitations" that "read well," "distorting—very creatively—an original beyond recognition" (1987, 171–73), prompting Nabokov to complain, "I wish he [Lowell] would stop mutilating dead and defenseless poets" (171–73).

We have been aware in making our choices that the "word for word" literalism of a "servile" literary translation, as Paz call it[15] (1992, 154)," however motivated by fidelity, is as likely to violate the intended meanings and effects of the original as to reproduce them in an alien tongue and literature. Such would have been the case had we not changed the taxonomic classification of bat as bird—manifestly in the title and first line of a poem which would have read "A bat or some other bird"—to the more amorphous bat as "creature," thus avoiding a misplaced emphasis in translation on a tacit but "incidental" (cf. Humboldt 1992, 56) understanding in the original, thus avoiding the jarring effects of taxonomic violation in English serving aesthetic or semantic purposes absent in the original. Ultimately, it is the "richness" (including ambiguity) in meaning and form that a "word for word" translation is likely to miss and mutilate, turning a literary work into a "glossary" (Paz 1992, 154), treating it as if it were a "cross-word puzzle" (Bonnefoy 1992, 188).

But we have also been aware of the hazards of shifting the center of gravity too far from the original author and work, even when it is done in the name of a deeper, more complex "fidelity," more responsive to the "strangeness" in the original and need for means to express that strangeness in its second language—"abusive" fidelity as Philip Lewis calls it (1985, 43), "resistant" translation, as it is called by Venuti (1992, 12). We have been aware of how abusive fidelity, unrestrained by a "love" for the original and a need to return to it (Humboldt 1992, 57–58; Nossack 1992, 228), may come to manifest more abuse than fidelity, at best serving the aesthetic, intellectual, and emotional needs of the translator-as-author, at worst presenting a "lowelized" translation without the aesthetic finish.

Such may be the extended example of "abusive translation" Sharon Willis holds up with admiration in Helene Cixous' "reading" in *Vivre L'Orange* of

---

15. "The Servile Path" is also the title of an essay by Nabokov on translating *Eugene Onegin* (1959, 97). But he uses it to a different purpose than Paz. To him "total accuracy and completeness" are clearly a primary goal for which he is willing to "sacrifice . . . every element of form save the iambic rhythm."

a Brazillian novel by Clarice Lispector, already translated into French by Clelia Pisa, and interspersed with translated passages in "broken English" (based on translations by Anne Liddel and Sarrah Cornell) to represent the strangeness of the original. The Brazilian work provides its translator the sort of ambiguous stimulus used in projective tests for playful but profound meditations, among other things, on the constitutive categories of her French-Algerian-woman-writer's identity, in which an Orange can stand for or translate into Iran. And why not? since "throughout the text" the orange can stand in for and translate into "everything: women, Jews, Iran, Clarice Inspector, writing, the body" (Willis 1992, 108).

This is not a protest by orange-loving Iranian translators who feel their feathers ruffled by the metamorphosis of *their* Iran to an orange: it makes sense, given the chains of associations and substitutions in Cixous' work and the preoccupations that motivate them (e.g., Iran: Oran: Algeria; the substitution O/I further "over-determined" by the "'O' in the 'I'" experienced by certain women of Cixous as "split" subjects; and then, the association, oranges: "oranjews" . . . (Willis, 111–12). But these remain palpably and pre-dominantly Cixous-the-author's preoccupations, intentions, and expressive acts, even though nourished by her idiosyncratic translations of the "lost orange" returned to her by a voice from Brazil (Clarice Lispector), her "birth-voice," *her* Iran (109, 111). It is the ratio of "abuse" in the "translation" viewed as translation, held up as a model for "abusive translation," antidote to "domesticating" the strange and alien in more conventional translations (Willis 1992, 108), that we find questionable.

Yet, in making our choices between different but seemingly unavoidable abuses, each with a different set of consequences, trying to choose the lesser of two or more "evils," we have been aware of the limitations and built-in contradictions in various "technical" attempts to *eliminate* abuse or what it represents—miscomprehension, miscommunication, misrepresentation, whether "willed" (for a variety of purposes, including "high" ones such as just discussed) or by necessity, as if it were possible to undo by some magical technique the "confusion of tongues" that followed the destruction of the tower of Babel. Clearly there are too many gaps to be filled by Nabokov's mountains of footnotes, "footnotes reaching up like sky-scrapers to the top of this or that page" (1992, 142), to compensate for the linguistic, musical, literary, cultural, social, and historical embeddedness of any poem, including *Eugene Onegin*, lost in translation. Clearly no amount of paraphrasing, glosses, commentaries, or "discussions"—the best we could do, Robert Frost suggested, given the nature of poetry as "that which gets lost in translation" (Burnshaw 1989, IX)—can enable us to experience a poem as it is experienced on its native/ alien ground, even when accom-

panied by dual language texts or readings (cf. the attempted "approxima-
tions," as Burnshaw himself calls them, in *The Poem Itself*).

Similarly, with the problem of "authenticity" in translation: representing
"foreignness" without sounding "foreign" (Humboldt 1992, 58); representing
the "foreign" in terms familiar enough for comprehension and aesthetic
appreciation without dissolving the differences that make it unique; repre-
senting "difference" without turning it into a caricature or something more
"distant" and exotic than originally perceived or intended.

Clearly there can be no complete or perfect solutions to these problems
outside fantasies of a literary "speaking in tongues" (likely to sound gib-
berish to the uninitiated) or the temporary "suspension of disbelief" when
immersed in the fictive world of a movie or a play (and sometimes a novel)
which allows us to "hear" and "understand" the conventionally broken Eng-
lish or foreign accent of a character as if they were spoken by a foreigner
speaking a foreign tongue—the Sergeant Shultz syndrome.

Clearly, in the quest for authenticity we can keep the center of gravity
of a translated poem *too close* to the language and aesthetics of the original,
letting their alien gravity twist and deform the syntax and idiom of the trans-
lation into a sort of "pidgin," as, for example, in the case of Nabokov's
authenticity-obsessed translation of *Eugene Onegin*. It may not be quite the
tribute to Pushkin Nabokov intended to have the great Russian poet recite
Onegin in a "pidgin English," as Guy Daniels calls it, replete with "man-dog-
bite" kind of deformations of English syntax[16] (1987, 172).

Clearly, however earnest the quest for authenticity in representing "dif-
ference" in translation, it cannot overcome the limitation that "difference"
cannot be represented or experienced directly (outside spirit-possession
and Star Trek fantasies of telepathy between individuals, groups, and
species); that, as a "construct" in an alien tongue and aesthetic tradition,
it can never be more than an "effect," an artifact, an "illusion"; that how
real or convincing such an illusion is experienced is as much a matter of
craftsmanship (poorly made illusions are less convincing) as of the reality
as such of the "difference" represented.

And clearly, too, however well-meaning the quest for authenticity in lit-
erary translation—that is, out of respect for the relative uniqueness of
strangers and the strangeness of their literature, and not out of a wish to con-
quer, colonize, cannibalize, or domesticate that strangeness, mutilate it to

---

16. Cf. Nabokov's own view, quoted by Steiner (1976, 315): "In fact, to my ideal of liter-
alism I have sacrificed everything (elegance, euphony, clarity, good taste, modern usage
and even grammar) that the dainty mimic prizes higher than truth."

fit one's own literary and cultural purposes or to prove one's own literary and cultural superiority (Nietzsche 1992, 68–69; Hugo Friedrich 1992, 12–13)— it does not preclude the possibility of consequences very different than intended. It does not preclude the possibility of turning great poems from a living poetic tradition into museum pieces, to be admired from the distance as linguistic, cultural, or historical "specimens"; or if appreciated as works of art, appreciated only for their reified and exaggerated difference, as caricatures or exotic objects; their "authenticity" serving as a funhouse mirror in which another people can find themselves by contrast, or as "nourishment" for their "expanding" consciousness, imagination, art.

And clearly, too, authenticity in translating a poem is not merely a matter of truth, of the kind that can be verified by checking a dictionary or cultural encyclopedia, but of shape, rhythm, music, intensity, flow—a matter of beauty. Keats's affirmation, "Beauty is Truth, Truth Beauty" applies to translating poetry as much as to anything else. And for the truth that is beauty, the ear is a primary measure, an organ of perception, an instrument with critical access to the heart, mind, and imagination. "The Translator with a tin ear," as Rabassa points out, "is as deadly as a tone-deaf musician . . . If a work sings in the original and does not in the translation, then the version is little more than a linear glossary" (1987, 82).

Here, too, the quest for authenticity, presents the literary translator with unavoidable but consequential choices: between copying, transcription, resonance, not of words and phrases, but form. Here the problems of literalism are compounded.

On the one hand, copying too closely the manifest "geometry" of a poem—its rhyme schemes, metrical segmentation, measurement of syllables, lines and stanzas—may clip the wings of a poem, preventing it from taking off aesthetically under an alien sky. Or to borrow Dryden's powerful metaphor, if poetic translation is like "dancing" on a tightrope, then this kind of literalism is like "dancing on ropes with fettered legs," in which a "a man may shun a fall by using caution," but at the cost of "gracefulness of motion" (1992, 18). On the other hand, turning a "tin ear" to how the manifest "geometry" of a poem resonates in its new literary and cultural environment may create not only a poem with less "gracefulness of motion," but with a beauty that feels and means differently than experienced or intended in its original setting—not in spite but because of the surface resemblance. And sometimes, as we shall see, "wrongly" copied music, may achieve a deeper, more encompassing resonance, than a literal copy.

We can see this in the loss of lightness and air in many translations of the great classics of Persian poetry by translators who, devoted as they may have been as translators (as proven, for example, by Nicholson's transla-

tion of the six books of Rumi's *Mathnawi*, and Arberry's two volume trans-
lations of Rumi's *Divan-e Shams*[17]), have tended to be more scholars than
poets in their translations. We often find in their works, clearly despite their
intentions and self-conscious fidelity, a heavy, musty air, not found in the
originals, an anachronism far more distant and reclusive than perceived in
their original setting—Rumi (d. 1273) is still very much a contemporary in
Iranian life, literature, culture; his translations sometimes have the stuffiness
of a Victorian relic, especially when resorting to Latin (sections in Nichol-
son, mostly in vol. 5) to cover up unseemly references to bodily functions
and sexuality.[18] We find poems at home in the widest range of profane and
sacred places in Iranian culture banished in translation to much more con-
fining spaces: the dusty shelves of the library, clutter on a scholar's desk,
collections of the rare and exotic in an antique store, esoterica for the lit-
erary and spiritual pedant. But is such a fate necessary, given the original
texts and the differences between culture? We think not.

Clearly the same texts can be translated differently, with different quo-
tients of beauty and resonant truth. And clearly they can find a different
place in their second home. Coleman Barks proves it. His poetic translations
of translations of Rumi (Moyne's, Nicholson's and Arberry's)—as unliteral
as they might be in idiom (American casual) and in form "American free
verse" as Barks likes to call it (Rourke 1998), with no attempt to replicate
Rumi's rhymes, but *adding* titles to poems, grouping them thematically in
separate books and chapters in a collection)—seem to have come a long
way in answering the "need" pointed out to him by fellow-American poet
Robert Bly in 1976: "These poems [a book of translations handed to Barks,
introducing him to Rumi for the first time] need to be released from their
cages" (Barks in interview with Moyers, in Moyers 1995, 46).

The "need(s)" addressed by Barks's metatranslations in "American free
verse," his infusion—or "release"—of truth-in-beauty/beauty-in-truth in
the older more inaccessible translations, seem to have been needs not
merely of the "caged" poems, but a constellation of needs in Rumi's new-

---

17. See Rumi 1925–40; 1968; 1979.

18. Paul Sprachman points out an interesting paradox: what Nicholson censored by
switching into Latin in his English translations he let stand in his Persian edition of the
Mathnawi (*Masnavi-e Maʾnavi*, Tehran: Amir Kabir, 1971), as if to acknowledge the different
literary and cultural niches the works occupy in their two literary and cultural environ-
ment, a far more specialized and restrictive niche in the second. For comments, transla-
tions, including Rumi verses in Latin and Rumi verses "suppressed" in Persian publica-
tions, see Sprachman 1995. For translations of translations of such verses, see Barks 1990.

found American home, aesthetic, literary, philosophical, and spiritual needs. We can see this in the phenomenal response to Barks's translations, his taped and live recitations, often with musical accompaniment, and sales of ten books (in our last count). Thus we find the announcement by *Publishers Weekly* that Rumi (by way of Barks) was the best-selling poet in America in 1994, with sales of *The Essential Rumi* exceeding 110,000 copies in three years (1995–98) by Harper San Francisco (Rourke 1998), and sales of all of Barks's translations of Rumi exceeding a quarter-million copies by 1997 (Marks 1997)—an all the more astonishing phenomena, as Marks points out, given poetry not being quite the national obsession in America, "where Pulitzer-winning poets often struggle to sell 10,000."

We can also appreciate the significance of problems in translating "gracefulness in motion," the meanings and feelings in (or evoked by) the form of a poem, by looking at a few attempts in translating form, that is, not Persian poems as such, but applying a form like the traditional ghazal to write poems in English.

On the one hand, in recent assimilations of the ghazal in America we can see how differently two literary and cultural environments can foreground different features of the same form and charge them with significance. This we can see, for example, in the heightened significance for many American poets enamored by the ghazal form of the thematic autonomy of ghazal lines, the gazelle-like "jumping" between lines; assimilating in this way a formal feature of a traditional and conservative poetic form in a "radical" but familiar aesthetics with a weakness for "discontinuity and unexpected juxtaposition," such as associated with surrealism (Doty 1996). However, from the perspectives of modern masters and revolutionists of the Persian ghazal, such as Lahuti and Behbahani, the same feature has more likely been viewed as confining than liberating, more a decorative mold to contain and hold back ideas and feelings, to keep them as bite-sized, easily digestible, formulas and clichés (such as the omnipresent tavern, the ever-complaining lover, the ever-cruel beloved), to keep them from reaching the "critical mass" needed to really move people, beyond the easy nods and interjections of recognition and approval.

On the other hand, we can see how the formalism as such of the traditional ghazal can occupy a different literary and cultural niche in its new home. Whereas in its Iranian setting we find the rigidity of the ghazal's patterned rhymes and meters (as well as formulaic themes and images) contributing to its predictability, "easy listening," memorization, fluency of performance, popularity as a genre, appeal to the masses as well as the literary elite. In its new home we find it occupying a far more specialized, restrictive niche, clearly not in the mainstream of contemporary American poetry, which seems to be drifting towards an increasing dissolution of manifest poetic forms into the more implicit, improvisatory forms of every day speech and prose (that is, if we do not consider, as would an anthropologist, the poetry that goes by another name, for example, the poetry of popular music, political demagogy, advertisements).

We find the formalism of traditional ghazal assimilated in a countercurrent: of genres on the margins, poets who for a variety of reasons—from self-conscious anachronism, conservatism, aesthetic contrariness, to craftsmanly fascination with challenges posed to one's skills and imagination by the restrictions and possibilities of a demanding or freshly "discovered" form—are unhappy with the freedoms of free verse. This is a niche in which traditional ghazal in its manifest formalism rubs shoulders with more traditional native forms, the sonnet, for example, or the sestina. But as mentioned earlier, for its American practitioners, the formal rigidity of the ghazal also promises a certain kind of freedom: like the Japanese *renga*, a liberating disconnectedness, in the relative thematic autonomy of its lines, the absence of "necessary, logical, progressive, narrative . . . connection" between them, hence the possibility of creating and perceiving a more subtle, "clandestine" order (Folsom 1995).

Conclusion

In translating these hundred or so poems by Simin Behbahani we have certainly experienced the "miseries" of translation, as Ortega y Gasset calls them (1992, 93).

We have felt the improbabilities of translation: hard enough between heart, mind, and tongue in the same person; hard enough between the senses and sensibilities of two persons in the same language and culture; utopian between different poems, literary traditions, languages and cultures. And however clear and well meant our intentions, we have felt the frustrations of "compromise," having too often to choose between the lesser of two evils, with losses inevitable in every choice.

Thus, even though "fidelity" in translation has been our ideal (that is, fidelity not of literalism in copying words and lines (Dryden 1992, 17–18), but of "transposition" (Riffaterre 1992, 205–7), "creative transposition" (Jakobson 1992, 151), "transmutation" (Paz 1992, 160); even though our "attitude" towards Behbahani and her poems has been dominated by love and respect, by a willingness to "walk the line" (Rabassa 1978, 83) set by *their* intentions and constraints (as understood by us), rather than by postmodern "vertical anxieties" (Gavronsky 1977, 55) over "authority," "originality" "creativity" and "influence" (Chamberlain 1992, 67–68)—anxieties expressed or acted out by critics and translators unwilling to play second fiddle to any "original author" or "original text," turf-war or zero-sum anxieties with a tendency to turn ugly, "Oedipal," "patricidal," "matricidal" (Johnston 1992, 51–52), even "cannibalistic" (Gavronsky 1977, 59–60)—we realize how much we have compromised this ideal. We may not have been Gavronsky's proud cannibals.[19] We may not have felt any relish in "abusive" translation (Lewis 1985; Willis 1992). But we realize there is blood on our translators' hands, however reluctant we have been to shed it. We are aware of the losses and mutilations caused by our translation, whether by choice, necessity, or circumstance.

Some of these have been inescapable losses and mutilations, having to do with the multilayered and distinctively textured—sometimes against the grain—embeddedness of the poet and her poems in the Persian language, in Iranian literature, culture, politics, and history; losses all the more irrecoverable for not being merely losses of facts, reducible to an inventory of linguistic, literary, cultural, and historical facts, but losses of Behbahani's distinctive engagement, resynthesis, and interpretation of these facts in her art, losses of the distinguishing alignments and friction in this engagement.

Some of these losses have been inescapable not because of the inherent impossibility of certain tasks but because of our limitations as translators and poets, for example, our insufficient mastery of speech genres and literary styles to create the illusion of a layered archaism or "patina," as Steiner calls it (1976, 341–49), which rather than break a poem's sense of contemporaneousness, can give it a sense of "interior" depth, historical rootedness, "cumulative tradition." Such layered archaisms—in idiom, syntax, form, literary, and cultural allusions (many to the Qoran, in verbatim quotations)—abound in Behbahani's poems, not making them distant or "out of touch" but infused with a gravity and urgency one associates with prayers, incantations, sacred narratives. We gave up early on trying to recreate such a vital "patina" in English. It was beyond our craftsmanship to approximate anything but simple caricatures of archaism, with little layering or interanimation of parts.

---

19. Of course, with Gavronsky's translator-cannibal, as with other cannibals engaged in ritualized cannibalism, it is not all destruction, making the "original" text and author and making them "disappear" "without a trace," but also a kind of "homage" and "reconciliation" through radical incorporation and revitalization (1977, 60–61). Despite his rhetorical and metaphorical overkill, i.e., dismissing "fidelity" as a form of oppressive "piety," as in Benedictine monastic vows of "chastity," "poverty" "obedience," Gavronsky allows for another kind of fidelity, not of the "crass duplication" of the original variety, but the *belles infidèles . . . that hope to be truer* (54, 59).

And some of these losses have been losses made by choice, albeit diffi-
cult choices, like those made at Solomon's court: willingness to lose one's
child or see it torn apart in a literalist application of justice. For us the dif-
ficult choice was to lose a signature-poetic feature of Behbahani's poetry,
the musical "geometry" of her new ghazal, in order to save it from a radi-
cal misplacement in its new home: a new "exoticism," aesthetic distance,
marginality. It wasn't that we believed the ghazal's manifest form could not
work in English—we have mentioned some notable experiments by Amer-
ican poets—but that, when it does, it means something very different, it
locates the ghazal in a very different aesthetic and cultural niche. Given the
vulnerability of any contemporary Iranian poetry to being perceived here as
strange or exotic—whether because of unfamiliarity, dearth of translations,
or political and cultural rift—and given the mood of the times which seems
to accentuate and reify differences, we felt it even more important not to
translate Behbahani's poems as more exotic and stylistically inaccessible
than they are in Persian. Hence our metamorphosis of the ghazal into free
verse: our decision to err on the side of "naturalization" rather than "exoti-
cization."[20]

Over all, our greatest cause for translators' misery—in part self-inflicted—
has been a stylistic "flattening" of Behbahani's poems in English, a flatten-
ing of idiom, speech genres, and styles: her crafted mixtures of the casual
and serious, the everyday and literary, the contemporary and archaic, the
traditional and modern, the familiar and strange, the easy and difficult. Our
translations have erred, however reluctantly, on the side of "fluency" (Venuti
1992, 4–5): reducing crafted turbulence, graininess, ambiguity. They have
erred on the side of images, argument, and narrative bearing a heavier bur-
den of meanings and feelings than does the complex music of Behbahani's
new ghazal. However diligently we have tried to maintain a bottom line in
our changes, to stop at the threshold of "differences that make a difference"
(Bateson 1972, 315), differences that significantly change the meanings and
feelings of a poem, we realize the contingency of this test for "significance."
It has not lightened our burden of responsibility or washed the blood stains
off our hands.

But it has not been all misery in translating Behbahani's poems. We have
also felt the exhilaration or "splendor" of translation, as Ortega y Gasset
calls it (1992, 108).

---

20. Of course, this problem or dilemma is not unique to translating Persian literature,
as Richard Jacquemond notes regarding French translations of Arabic literature, under
the subheading, "Between Exoticization and Naturalization" (1992, 150–55).

We have experienced the fact that formidable as barriers of distance and difference may be in language, literature, and culture, they are not impermeable. Messages can go through, though transposed, reenacted, interpreted (Ramanujin 1989, 61–62). And poems, Robert Frost's doubts not withstanding, present a special promise as means and ends in this breaking through: for the intensified palpability in them of feelings and meanings, through an "intensification of form," figurative language, and analogy (Friedrich 1979, 458–68); for the palpable "interiorization" in them of significant linguistic, literary, and cultural "contexts" (Ramanujin 1989, 61); for the "gist"-like inscriptions in them of an individual poet's "deep concerns, attitudes, and symbols" as well as those of the poet's community brought into play or in various ways engaged in her poem (Friedrich 1996, 39). It may be that as dreams constitute a "royal path to the unconscious," poems constitute a "royal path" to "other" versions of reality, aesthetic and cultural sensibilities, a royal path for cutting through distance and difference.

We have experienced in our wrestling with the "confusion of tongues" that the destruction of the Tower was not all a curse.

We have come to experience in palpable, practical terms the limits of it as a punishment. However imperfect or incomplete have been our translations as acts of communication between languages and cultures, they have forced into our consciousness the existence and necessity of "universals" in language and human experience (Ramanujin 1989, 60; Friedrich 1979, 455–58); of bonds and affinities that lie deeper than the walls and chasms that separate individuals and groups (Benjamin 1992, 75), without which, however dimly perceived or hypothesized, no communication would be possible, including these translations.

Not only limited as a punishment, we have also come to see this "confusion of tongues" in terms of its blessings—not just for creating a need for translators, practicing a necessary but impossible craft but for more consequential reasons, increasing exponentially our freedoms as human beings to think, feel, imagine, act, create and understand, to the extent that these capacities are based on, or affected by, language. Language by itself is like a secreted skin that may bind us but also prevent us from being completely confined by the givenness and inevitability of an empirical world (Steiner 1976, 473)—it gives, us, among other things, the "negative capability" of seeing things as they could be, not just the way they are; it allows us to question and criticize and conjure up alternative worlds, even to act out imaginary schemes, making them real. However, by all of us not being "lodged" inside the same "language skin" (Steiner 1976, 473)—as we would be, had not the Babelian destruction sentenced us to linguistic "individuation" (473)—the possibilities opened and limited by language are multiplied astronomically, limited ultimately by the number of existing and potential idiolects, each a world with a difference that could potentially make a difference.

Translation allows us to tap this potential. There is the thrill in translating a poem of seeing different possibilities of beauty and meaning emerging with each turn of the linguistic and cultural kaleidoscope. If there is any life in a poem—only dead poems are really "completed" (Vallery 1992, 122)—there is the thrill in translation of seeing its "renewal," "abundant flowering" in an alien landscape (Benjamin 1992, 73–74). And there is the consolation of other potentials to be realized by other translations, multiple translations, of the same work in the same landscape (Oretga y Gasset 1992, 110). There is consolation for the guilt-stricken translator with blood-stained hands—and which translator, however "adequate" to the task (Steiner's definition of "fidelity" [1976, 396]) has not?—in the possibility that the stains are those on the hands of a midwife who has assisted the rebirth of a poem. For the translator guilt-stricken at having uprooted a poem from its native soil, there is consolation in the potential "afterlife" (or afterlives)—in translation(s)—of a poem (Benjamin 1992, 73); there is hope in believing that he or she has not played the role of the Azrael, the Angel of Death, separating soul and body from a poem, or Charon, carrying the souls of murdered poems to the land of dead verse, but of a shaman initiating a poem in a translinguistic and cultural rite of passage. More down to Earth, the translator may dare believe in the significance of his or her work as a moral-political act: letting through and deciphering the tapping on the wall; functioning as "a kind of underground radio station used by partisans of humanity throughout the world to send news of their endangered existence" (Nossack 1992, 234); allowing a counterpoint to the doublespeak, jingoism, bombast, hectoring, hot air, empty chatter, and platitudes blaring on "megaphones" (234) and other instruments for the propagation of silence within and between us.

Bibliography

Ahmad, Aijaz, ed. 1971. *Ghazals of Ghalib: Versions From Urdu*. New York: Columbia University Press.

Akhavan-Sales, Mehdi. 1956. *Zemestan [Winter]*. Tehran: Entesharat-e Morvarid.

———. 1970. *Majmuʾeh-ye Maqalat* [Collected Essays]. Tehran: Entesharat-e Tus.

Barks, Coleman. 1990. *Delicious Laughter: Rambunctious Teaching Stories from the Mathnawi of Jalaluddin Rumi*. Athens Ga.: Maypop.

Barks, Coleman, et al., trans. 1995. *The Essential Rumi*. San Francisco: Harper.

Bateson, Gregory. 1972. *Steps Towards an Ecology of Mind*. New York: Ballantine.

Behbahani, Simin. 1956. *Jayeh Pa* [*Footprints*]. Tehran: Kanun-e Maʾrefat.

———. 1957. *Chelcheragh* [*Candelabrum*]. Tehran: Entesharat-e Amir Kabir.

———. 1963 [1991]. *Marmar* [*Marble*]. Tehran: Entesharat-e Zavvar.

———. 1973. *Rastakhiz*. [*Resurrection*]. Tehran: Entesharat-e Zavvar.

———. 1981. *Khati ze Sorʾat va az Atash* [*A Trajectory of Speed and Fire*]. Tehran: Entesharat-e Zavvar.

———. 1983. *Dasht-e Arzhan* [*Plains of Arzhan*]. Tehran: Entesharat-e Zavvar.

———. 1992. *Kaghazin Jameh* [*Clothes Like Paper*]. San Jose, Calif.: Nashr-e Zamaneh.

———. 1993. "Ta Toluʾi Talaʾi Cheshm Beh Rah Darim" ["We Await the Golden Dawn"]. *Nimeye Digar* 2, no. 1: 167–76.

———. 1995. *Yek Daricheh-ye Azadi* [*A Window to Freedom*]. Tehran: Entehsarat-e Sokhan.

———. 1996. *Ba Qalb-e Khod Cheh Kharidam, Gozineh-ye Qesseh-ha va Yad-ha*. [*What Did I Buy with My Heart: Selection of Stories and Remembrances*]. Los Angeles: Ketab.

Benjamin, Walter. 1992 [1923]. "The Task of the Translator." In *Theories of Translation: An Anthology of Essays from Dryden to Derrida*, edited by Rainer Shulte and John Biguenet, 71–82. Chicago: Univ. of Chicago Press.

Bonnefoy, Yves. 1992 [1989]. "Translating Poetry." In *Theories of Translation: An Anthology of Essays from Dryden to Derrida*, edited by Rainer Shulte and John Biguenet, 186–92. Chicago: Univ. of Chicago Press.

Burnshaw, Stanley, ed. 1989. *The Poem Itself*. First Touchstone edition. New York: Simon and Shuster.

Chamberlain, Lori. 1992. "Gender and the Metaphorics of Translation." In *Rethinking Translation: Discourse, Subjectivity, Ideology*, edited by Lawrence Venuti, 57–74. New York: Routledge.

Clark, Katerina, and Michael Holquist. 1984. *Mikhail Bakhtin*. Cambridge: Harvard Univ. Press.

Daniels, Guy. 1987 [1970]. "The Lot of the Translator." In *The World of Translation*. Proceeding of the Conference on Literary Translations, 167–74. New York: PEN American Center, May.

Dehkhoda, Ali Akbar. 1960. *Loghatnameh*. Tehran: Univ. of Tehran Press.

Doty, Gene. 1996. "When I Say 'Ghazal,' I Mean 'Ghuzzle.'" In *Lynx* 11 (2 June 1996), revised by Gener Doty (n.d., n.p.) 25 prgs. Posted on the internet, http://www.umr.deu/~gdoty/poems/ghazals.html, 20 June 1998.

Dryden, John. 1992 [1680]. "On Translation." In *Theories of Translation: An*

Anthropology of Essays from Dryden to Derrida, edited by Rainer Shulte and John Biguenet, 17–31. Chicago: Univ. of Chicago Press.

Ejxenbaum, Boris M. 1971 [1927]. "The Theory of The Formal Method." In *Readings in Russian Poetics: Formalist and Structuralist Views*, edited by Ladislav Matejka and Krystyna Pomorska, 56–65. Cambridge, Mass.: MIT Press.

Empson, William. 1960. *Seven Types of Ambiguity*. New York: New Directions.

E'tesami, Parvin. 1985. *A Nightingale's Lament: Selections from the Poems and Fables of Parvin E'tesami*. Translated by Heshmat Moayyad and Margaret A. Madlung. Lexington, Ky.: Mazda.

Farrokhzad, Forugh. 1974. *Iman Biavarim be Aghaz-e Fasl-e Sard* [Let us believe in the dawn of a cold season]. Tehran: Morvarid.

Fesharaki, Mohammad. 1993. "Az Khalil ta Simin: az Doroshti-ye Jang ta Nashakiba-'iyeh Jan" [From Khalil to Simin: From the coarsness of war to spiritual anxiety]. *Nimeye Digar* 2, no. 1: 67–82.

Folsom, Eric. 1995. "Commentary on Ghazals." In *Ghazal*. Posted by AHA Books on the internet, (n.p.) 5 prgs., http://www.faximum.com/aha.d/ghazal.html#comment, 20 June 1998.

Friedrich, Hugo. 1992 [1965]. "On the Art of Translation." In *Theories of Translation: An Anthology of Essays from Dryden to Derrida*, edited by Rainer Shulte and John Biguenet, 11–16. Chicago: Univ. of Chicago Press.

Friedrich, Paul. 1979. "Poetic Language and Imagination: A Reformulation of the Sapir Hypothesis." In *Language, Context and the Imagination: Essays by Paul Friedrich*, edited by Paul Friedrich, 441–512. Stanford, Calif.: Stanford Univ. Press.

———. 1996. "The Culture in Poetry and Poetry in Culture." In *Culture/Contexture: Exploration in Anthropology and Literary Studies*, edited by E. Daniel Valentine and Jeffrey M. Peck, 37–57. Berkeley: Univ. of California Press.

Gavronsky, Serge. 1977. "The Translator: From Piety to Cannibalism." *Substance* 16: 53–62.

Ghanoonparvar, M. R. 1984. *Prophets of Doom: Literature as a Socio-political Phenomenon in Modern Iran*. Lanham, Md.: Univ. Press of America.

Hafez, Shams-eddin Mohammad. 1983. *Divan-e Hafez, Ghazaliat*. Vol. 1, edited by Parviz Natel Khanlari. Tehran: Entesharat-e Kharazmi.

Humboldt, Wilhelm von. 1992. [1816]. "From the Introduction to His Trnaslation of *Agammemnon*." Translated by Sharon Sloan. In *Theories of Translation: An Anthology of Essays from Dryden to Derrida*, edited by Rainer Shulte and John Biguenet, 55–59. Chicago: Univ. of Chicago Press.

Jacquemond, Richard. 1992. "Translation and Cultural Hegemony: The Case of French-Arabic Translation." In *Rethinking Translation: Discourse, Subjectivity, Ideology,* edited by Lawrence Venuti, 139–58. New York: Routledge.

Jakobson, Roman. 1992 [1959]. "On Linguistic Aspects of Translation." In *Theories of Translation: An Anthology of Essays from Dryden to Derrida,* edited by Rainer Shulte and John Biguenet, 144–51. Chicago: Univ. of Chicago Press.

Johnston, John. 1992. "Translation as Simulacrum." In *Rethinking Translation: Discourse, Subjectivity, Ideology,* edited by Lawrence Venuti, 42–56. New York: Routledge.

Karimi-Hakkak, Ahmad. 1995. *Recasting Persian Poetry: Scenarios of Poetic Modernity in Iran.* Salt Lake City: Univ. of Utah Press.

Lewis, E. Philip. 1985. "The Measure of Translation Effects." In *Difference in Translation,* edited by Joseph Graham, 31–62. Ithaca, N.Y.: Cornell Univ. Press.

Marks, Alexandra. 1997. "Persian Poet Top Seller in America." *Christian Science Monitor,* Nov. 25, pp. 1, 4.

McDowell, Bart. 1970. *The Gypsies: Wanderers of the World.* National Geographic Society.

Milani, Farzaneh. 1992. *Veils and Words: The Emerging Voices of Iranian Women Writers.* Syracuse: Syracuse Univ. Press.

———. 1993. "Moshti Por Setareh" [A fist full of stars]. *Nimeye Digar* 2, no. 1: 37–62.

———. 1997. "The Life and Poetry of Simin Behbahani." Unpublished manuscript, delivered at Georgetown Univ., Oct. 25.

Moyers, Bill. 1995. *The Language of Life: A Festival of Poets.* New York. Doubleday.

Nabokov, Vladimir. 1959. "The Servile Path." In *On Translation,* edited by Arthur Reuben, 97–110. Cambridge, Mass.: Harvard Univ. Press.

———. 1992 [1955]. "Problems of Translation: Onegin in English." In *Theories of Translation: An Anthology of Essays from Dryden to Derrida,* edited by Rainer Shulte and John Biguenet, 127–43. Chicago: Univ. of Chicago Press.

Najmabadi, Afsaneh. 1995. "The Eclipse of the Female Sun: Masculine State, Fantasmatic Females, and National Erasures." Paper presented at the Middle East Institute, Columbia Univ., Oct. 26.

Nietzsche, Friedrich. 1992 [1882]. "On the Problem of Translation." In *Theories of Translation: An Anthology of Essays from Dryden to Derrida,* edited by Rainer Shulte and John Biguenet, 68–70. Chicago: Univ. of Chicago Press.

Nossack, Hans Erich. 1992 [1965]. "Translating and Being Translated." In *The-*

ories of Translation: An Anthology of Essays from Dryden to Derrida, edited by Rainer Shulte and John Biguenet, 228–38. Chicago: Univ. of Chicago Press.

Ortega y Gasset, José. 1992 [1947]. "The Misery and the Splendor of Translation." In *Theories of Translation: An Anthology of Essays from Dryden to Derrida*, edited by Rainer Shulte and John Biguenet, 93–112. Chicago: Univ. of Chicago Press.

Parvizi, Rasul. 1978. "Luli-ye Sarmast" [Intoxicated gypsy]. In *Luli-ye Sarmast*, 17–53. Tehran: Entesharat-e Javidan.

Paz, Octavio. 1992 [1971]. "Translation: Literature and Letters." In *Theories of Translation: An Anthology of Essays from Dryden to Derrida*, edited by Rainer Shulte and John Biguenet, 152–62. Chicago: Univ. of Chicago Press.

Rabassa, Gregory. 1987 [1970]. "The Ear in Translation." In *The World of Translation*. Proceedings of the Conference on Literary Translations, 81–86. New York: PEN American Center, May.

Ramanujin, A. K. 1989. "On Translating a Tamil Poem." In *The Art of Translation: Voices from the Field*, edited by Rosanna Warren, 47–93. Boston: Northeastern Univ. Press.

Riffaterre, Michael. 1992 [1985]. "Transposing Presuppositions of the Semiotics of Literary Translation." In *Theories of Translation: An Anthology of Essays from Dryden to Derrida*, edited by Rainer Shulte and John Biguenet, 204–17. Chicago: Univ. of Chicago Press.

Rourke, Mary. 1998. "The Mysterious Hold of a 13th-Century Mystic: An Academic Took License and Translations of Rumi's Verse Took Off." *Los Angeles Times*, Saturday, June 20.

Rumi, Jalaluddin. 1925–40. *The Mathnawi of Jalaluddin Rumi*. 8 vols. Translated by R. A. Nicholson. London: Lusaz.

———. 1968. *The Mystical Poems of Rumi*. Translated by A. J. Arberry. Chicago: Univ. of Chicago Press.

———. 1979. *Mystical Poems of Rumi: Second Selection, Poems 201–400*. Translated by A. J. Arberry. Persian Heritage Series, no. 23, edited by Ehsan Yarshater. Boulder, Colo.: Westview Press, 1979.

———. 1990. *Delicious Laughter: Rambunctious Teaching Stories from the Mathnawi*, versions by Coleman Barks. Athens, Ga.: Maypop Books.

———. 1995. *The Essential Rumi*. Translations by Coleman Barks, et al. San Francisco: Harper.

Sadr-eddin-e Elahi. 1997. "Interview with Simin Behbahani." In *Iran-Shenasi* 1997, no. 1: 124–25.

Sepehri, Sohrab. 1989. *Hasht Ketab* [Eight books]. Tehran: Ketabkhaneh-ye Tahuri.

Shamlu, Ahmad. 1980. *Taraneha-ye Kuchak-e Ghorbat* [Short poems of exile]. Tehran: Maziar.

Sprachman, Paul. 1995. *Suppressed Persian: An Anthology of Forbidden Literature.* Costa Mesa, Calif.: Mazda.

Steiner, George. 1976. *After Babel: Aspects of Language and Translation.* New York: Oxford Univ. Press.

Sway, Marlene. 1988. *Familiar Strangers: Gypsy Life in America.* Chicago: Univ. of Illinois.

Turner, Victor. 1970. *The Forest of Symbols: Aspects of Ndembu Ritual.* Ithaca, N.Y.: Cornell Univ. Press.

Tynjanov. 1971 [1929]. "On Literary Evolution." In *Readings in Russian Poetics: Formalist and Structuralist Views,* edited by Ladislav Matejka and Krystyna Pomorska, 66–78. Cambridge, Mass.: MIT Press.

Valery, Paul. 1992 [1953]. "Variations on the *Ecloques*." Translated by Denise Folliot. In *Theories of Translation: An Anthology of Essays from Dryden to Derrida,* edited by Rainer Shulte and John Biguenet, 113–26. Chicago: Univ. of Chicago Press.

Venuti, Lawrence. 1992. "Introduction." In *Rethinking Translation: Discourse, Subjectivity, Ideology,* edited by Lawrence Venuti, 1–17. New York: Routledge.

Vesey-Fitzgerald, Brian. 1973. *Gypsies of Britain: An Introduction to Their History.* New Abbott, Devon, U.K.: David & Charles.

Willis, Sharon. 1992. "Mistranslation, Missed Translation: Helene Cixous' Vivre L'Orange." In *Rethinking Translation: Discourse, Subjectivity, Ideology,* edited by Lawrence Venuti, 106–19. New York: Routledge.

Yushij, Nima. 1963. *Bargozideh-ye Ashʾar* [Selection of Poems]. Tehran: Sazeman-e Ketabha-ye Jibi.